contents

"Don't waste time wondering if you're doing it right. Read this book. Then you'll be armed with the knowledge of the pros."

— **John Larroquette, Actor/Producer**

"Rona and Monika have mentored and taught hundreds of students from all over the world who have passed through UCLA Extension's Department of Entertainment Studies and Performing Arts Department's program. The information they impart on how to develop projects is an invaluable foundation for anyone interested in pursuing a career in the entertainment business."

— **Jane Kagan, former Chair, Department of
Entertainment Studies & Performing Arts,
UCLA Extension**

"For writers, directors, aspiring development gladiators about to enter the death-sport known as the movie business, Edwards and Skerbelis give away the 'How-To-Crush-Hollywood' playbook."

— **Adam Novak, Story Editor, William Morris Agency**

"Rona and Monika bring a wealth of experience to the development process from both the studio and independent producer's perspective. Having taught 'development' for many years, they know their stuff so it was only natural they'd write a book about it, a book that should be read by everyone who wants to understand the process that movies don't just get made."

— **Fern Field, Writer/Director/Producer,**
Monk, Heartsounds, Kane & Abel, Counterstrike

"I loved it. This book is a must-read for anyone entering the treacherous waters of feature film development."

— **Elizabeth Hunter, Writer,** *Beauty Shop,*
The Fighting Temptations, L- Word, ER

"Rona and Monika have walked the walk and talked the talk. They've taught development, worked in development, gotten movies produced, and now they've written the first book of its kind on the development process from coverage to screen. This book should be on every filmmaker's bookshelf."

— **Howard Cohen, Co-President of
Roadside Attractions**

"This book doesn't just stop at who's who and how the development process works at studios, production companies, and agencies, it also provides insight on how to land that first job, how to find new ideas and the necessary attributes required to work in the entertainment industry."

— **Zanne Devine, Producer,** *Mardi Gras, Easy A,*
The Guardian

"Given everything Rona and Monika know about Hollywood, they should be heading up development at a studio, and if you buy this book, someday you might too!"

— **Anne Beatts, Emmy Award-Winning**
Writer/Producer, *Square Pegs, Saturday Night Live*

"Monika and Rona really know their stuff. I hope many aspiring filmmakers and executives read this book and learn how to collaborate to make better films."

— **Eric d'Arbeloff, Producer,** *Trick, Lovely & Amazing,*
Co-President of Roadside Attractions

"Before you make it, you first have to sell it and develop it. Those of us already in film refer to this process as 'development hell'. If you don't want to find yourself in "development hell", read this book. It will add years to your life."

— **Anne Carlucci, Producer,**
Guilt by Association, Sex & Mrs. X.

"Rona Edwards and Monika Skerbelis are the only angels in development hell. Read this book if you don't want to get burned."

— **Skip Press, Author,**
The Ultimate Writer's Guide to Hollywood

"As only insiders can do, Monika and Rona take the reader inside the esoteric world of script development and make it completely understandable. Based upon their considerable experience, they've been able to shed light on a process that can be mystifying and frustrating. Hooray for the authors and their ability to guide us through the creative maze with clarity, skill and grace."

— **Michael Serafin, Studio Story Analyst**

"*I Liked It, Didn't Love It* should be a prerequisite for anyone and everyone who is developing or writing screenplays, shedding light on an area that is the least understood in the business."

— **Nana Greenwald, Producer,** *North Country,*
former President of Kopelson Entertainment

"*I Liked It, Didn't Love It* tells you who does what in the world of film development and provides an in depth look at how to get your novel, screenplay, or idea developed into a movie. A must read for directors, producers, screenwriters, assistants and development execs!"

— **Cari-Esta Albert, Producer,**
The Truth About Cats & Dogs

"I Liked It, Didn't Love It"

SCREENPLAY DEVELOPMENT FROM THE INSIDE OUT

SECOND EDITION

RONA EDWARDS & MONIKA SKERBELIS

I LIKED IT, DIDN'T LOVE IT, 2nd Edition
Screenplay Development From the Inside Out
Copyright © 2009 Rona Edwards & Monika Skerbelis

Edwards Skerbelis Entertainment (ESE)
264 S. La Cienega Blvd, Suite 1052
Beverly Hills, CA 90211
Phone 310-278-4484
www.esentertainment.net

Second Edition: ISBN 978-0-61531-655-0
Printed in the United States of America
10 9 8 7 6 5 4 3 2

Cover design by zekeDESIGN
Book design by Carla Green

Library of Congress Cataloging-in-Publication Data

    Edwards, Rona
    I liked it, didn't love it : screenplay development from the inside out / Rona Edwards, Monika Skerbelis
       p.   cm.
    ISBN 1-58065-062-7
    1. Motion picture authorship. I. Skerbelis, Monika. II. Title

    PN1996.E39 2005
    808.2'3—dc22   2004058606

Chapter heading cartoons by Maratta from *Silent Pictures* by Maratta, courtesy of Katie Maratta. All rights reserved.

Black Dog coverage Copyright 2005 by Universal Studios Licensing LLLP. Courtesy of Universal Studios Licensing LLLP. All Rights Reserved.

"What Happens to a Screenplay" illustration courtesy of Kay Reindl.

Books may be purchased in bulk at special discounts for promotional or educational purposes. Inquiries for sales and distribution, textbook adoption, foreign language translation, editorial, and rights and permissions inquiries should be addressed to: Rona Edwards or Monika Skerbelis, Edwards Skerbelis Entertainment (ESE), 264 S. La Cienega Blvd., Suite 1052, Beverly Hills, CA 90211 or send email to info@esentertainment.net

acknowledgements

There are so many people to thank not only for helping us with this book but also for encouraging us through the years. With so many people whom we've met on the path to writing this book, we only hope our list acknowledges their contributions to the writing and to our lives which brought us to this point.

Rona would first and foremost like to thank her family and loved ones: my late mother and father, Ruth and Edward Goldstein, who always encouraged me to go beyond my dreams, and for their love. To Sue and Al Bornstein who have always been there for me on every level. Special thanks and love also go to Robin Schreer for not only her editing prowess, but also the laughter, the movies, the caring, and for seeing the best in me. Deepest appreciation and love go to Jude "j" Garrison for encouraging me, teaching me about life, freeing me to see the many possibilities, and lifting me up to be a better person. I have been blessed. To Monika, without you there would be no book, no class, and life would be a lot less interesting! Your support and friendship mean everything to me. To my other friends whose encouragement keeps me going—Anne Beatts (we've been a part of each other's journey for many years), Sandy Siegel (my "Buffy" pal), Debbie and David Tenzer, Mae Woods, Linda Graeme, Barbara Multer-Wellin, Jeanne Hartman, Nana Greenwald, Jeff Gelberg, Doug Stelzner, Richard and Marina Pierce—you've all known me a long, long time and you've always believed in me. Thanks go to Carolyn Broner for introducing Monika and I, thus setting us off on this path. Thanks to Beth McElhenny, Meredith Ralston, and Marianne Moore, former students, now friends, who have helped me time and again. To the ladies who lunch, thanks for all your support the past 12 years! To my clients who are also my friends, Bradley Rand Smith for his beautiful writing but also his undying friendship, to Aaron Mason and Tom Gates whose optimism still amazes me, to Eric Williams whose talent overflows in both writing and design, to Ross Schwartz (for friendship and wine appreciation), James Moseley, Jon Moseley, Chris Schefter, Chris Fritschi, and Mathew Carver, thanks for sticking with me. I believe in you too!

Thanks to Fern Field and Annie Carlucci for teaching me the business and how to work with writers and executives and, above all—how to tell a good story! To John Larroquette for giving me the opportunity to work for someone who has integrity and smarts. To Dave Collins for buying my projects and giving sound advice. To my attorney, Linda Lichter, who has always given me the time even when we weren't making a lot of money!

Monika would like to thank her family: my mother, Erika and father, Herbert and his wife, Anna, brother, John, sister-in-law Shirley, nephew Jesse and my nieces, Staci and Cayce for their support and love starting from the day I told them I wanted to work in the film industry. I would like to express my deep affection and appreciation to Tina Miller for her encouragement and being by my side. Thanks are also given to my mentors, Lora Lee for opening the door and showing me the ropes, and the unstoppable Cari-Esta Albert, for her friendship and constant guidance over the years. I'm also grateful to my friends who have stuck by my side, Elizabeth Hunter for the hikes, drinks, and infinite wisdom, Rosanne Korenberg for the spirit to travel, taking me further than I would have imagined, Robin Schreer, Harrison Reiner, Victoria Arch, Zsuzsa Londe, Carolyn Broner, Laurie Woodrow, Kathy Miller Kelly, Trisha O'Brien, Jean Bock, Nicholas Caron, and Zanne, Howard and Eric for their friendship along with all the students who have become friends over the years. To Liisa Primack, Jill Sweeney, Valerie Bessler who have known me longer than anybody and their love has always been there for me. But above all,

I want to thank Rona Edwards for her unfailing friendship, encouragement, creativity, and our empire we are building.

Together, we would like to thank Linda Seger and Skip Press whose advise and friendship has been enormously appreciated. Thanks to Robyn Snyder and Martin Gostanian for contributing so much information on the television movie and, of course, to the Museum of Television and Radio for putting us in contact with Martin. To the Writers Guild of America West Library, the Margaret Herrick Library, and staff of the Academy of Motion Picture Arts and Sciences who were so helpful in our research as well as Kevin Wyatt at Baseline StudioSystems and the countless people we've spoken to at Film Festivals and online services in order to make a coherent list of resources. Thanks to Jeanette Brackeen and the Producers Guild of America for helping us define a "producer." To Bob Fisher and the American Society of Cinematographers for allowing us to photograph Edison's Kinetoscope. Special thanks also go to those who answered questions: Richard Fischoff, Ted Dobb, Michael Hernandez, John Boswell, Holly Welch, Rey Luce, Kit Stoltz, Karl Schanzer, Kim Adelman, Andrea McCall, Teresa Wayne, and to Kay Reindl for her drawing, as well as all our friends at UCLA Extension: Jane Kagan, Allison Reeds, Judith Chlipala, Pascale Halm of Entertainment Studies for Performing Arts.

We are also deeply grateful to the following industry professionals who have graced our development classes with their wisdom by being guest speakers, adding significantly to the content of this book: Cari-Esta Albert, producer; Jason Abril, executive; Kelly Allen, reader/assistant; Victoria Arch, writer; Anne Beatts, writer; Ashley Berns, manager; Nicholas Bogner, executive; Howard Cohen, agent/producer; Eric d'Arbeloff, producer; Carr D'Angelo, executive/producer; Debbie Deuble, agent; Zanne Devine, executive; Gloria Fan, executive; Pierce Gardner, writer; Alan Gasmer, agent; Emile Gladstone, agent; Jennifer Good, agent; Nana Greenwald, executive; Marc Haimes, executive; Peter Heller, producer/manager; Barry Isaacson, executive; John Kapral, executive; Lenny Kornberg, executive; Spencer Krull, writer; Kurt Kubena, executive; David Madden, producer/executive; Erin Maher, writer/story analyst/story department; Sonny Mahli, executive; Gina Matthews, producer/manager; Joel Millner, agent; Adam Novak, story editor; Suzanne Patmore, executive; Sheryl Peterson, agent; Harrison Reiner, story analyst; Kay Reindl, writer/story department; Lucy Rimalower, executive; Michael Serafin, story analyst; John Soriano, story analyst; Betsy Stahl, producer;

Catherine Tarr, story editor; Ed Wacek, executive; Matt Wall executive; Jim Wedaa, producer; Eric Williams, writer.

And to all our former students who have helped shape and validate our teachings, making this book a reality.

A special debt of gratitude and thanks goes to Jeff Black for his support and our amazing and wonderful editors, Steve Atinsky and Lauren Rossini, Zeke Zielinski for the book cover design, Carla Green for the book layout, and Katie Maratta for her delightful and all too true cartoons. Their enthusiasm for what we were trying to accomplish helped propel us to the completion of this book.

— Rona Edwards & Monika Skerbelis
Hollywood, 2005

We've received so many letters and emails from readers expressing how this book has helped them achieve their dreams and get ahead in Hollywood. While the industry has changed economically, one thing remains the same, there will always be stories to tell and there will always be a development process. We hope we can help more of you with this second edition and want to wish you the best on your creative journey.

— Rona Edwards & Monika Skerbelis
Hollywood, 2009

when hollywood beats a good idea to death

introduction:
welcome to the world
of development

Since the beginning of time, human beings have yearned to communicate. First, they did so by using their hands and sounds. Over time, sounds became words and words formed sentences. Once language was established, man loved to tell a good yarn. They were so fascinated by their own stories, they began to draw them on the walls of their cave dwellings, which allowed them to convey their lives to others. Thus began the love affair with storytelling. We've come a long way from those days. The cavemen would be fascinated to know that their storytelling inspired future generations and that stories would be written and sold as books, and some of those books and stories would become plays. With the advent of the twentieth century, those books, plays, and stories would eventually turn into movies—giving birth to a whole new form of writing and storytelling called screenwriting.

There are many books written about screenwriting. They talk about structure, characters, and dialogue. They talk about how to sell your screenplay to Hollywood. They tell of case studies about movies that have already been produced and give advice on whom to contact and where to learn filmmaking. For the most part, these books are very helpful. But none of them have taken the mystery known as the "Hollywood development system," and clarified it...until now. We intend to unravel this mystery by showing you an in-depth look at what happens behind-the-scenes when a script leaves the writer's hands and is submitted to a studio and/or production company. What *is* "development?" How does it help the movie? Why is it necessary? Who are the people you need to know about? What are the underpinnings of the day-to-day work done by hard-working personnel known in this industry as readers, development executives, and production executives? The following chapters will shed light on all those questions for those who are new to the business, and further enlighten those who have already had the pleasure of journeying through the sacred creative halls at a film studio, television network, or production company. Today, audiences are savvier to the inner-workings of filmmaking thanks to television shows like *Entertainment Tonight*, *Access Hollywood*, and insightful behind-the-scenes profiles incorporated into DVD "value-added material." They have heard about development, but they don't really know what that word means. Their interest may have been piqued by movies that allude to the process of Hollywood—films such as Billy Wilder's *Sunset Boulevard* (1950), or Robert Altman's *The Player* (1992). But, even so, development remains a mystery to most people and is viewed as a curse by the majority of writers.

Working in development for many years, at both the studio and independent producer level, we have given seminars and workshops on "pitching" and "feature film development" at writing conferences, film festivals, and on discussion panels worldwide. We have also taught a very successful course at UCLA Extension for the past ten years titled *Introduction to Feature Film Development.* Our individual experiences differ from one another in that one of us worked solely for the studio system while the other worked solely for independent producers. In our classes and seminars, this difference allows us to bring a "yin and a yang" perspective to the development process. This gives our students a wider view of the film business and encourages them to think outside of the box. We have nurtured and championed many writers in our respective careers as executives and producers. We want this book to be an extension of that encouragement.

If you are a filmmaker, writer, a person wanting to break into the Hollywood clique, or even someone who aspires to become a development executive or reader, this book will help you understand the "who, what, where, how, and whys" of a system that has been working for over one hundred years. Sure, the process has evolved to a certain degree, but the basic principles remain the same. A script is sold, or optioned, to a studio and/or production company. However, it doesn't just get made "as is." A studio, producers, and other individuals connected to the project have countless thoughts as to what will make the script's storyline, characters, and dialogue work better. In order to gather all these opinions and suggestions for rewriting the screenplay into one cohesive set of development notes, someone was needed to organize it—someone who had a handle on the story and yet would still keep the goals of the studio and/or production company in mind. Thus, the development executive was born.

The film business is like no other; it's seductive as it dangles the carrot of success in front of you. But, make no mistake, it's not an easy journey. You have to work very hard. There is no such thing as an overnight success. So while you will learn about the process of development and even get a glimpse of how to get started in that aspect of the business, you must know that to succeed means putting your nose to the grindstone, being persistent, and focusing on your goals till you reach them. We hope we can be influential and helpful in your success!

1

"I Thought Movies Just Got Made!"

defining development

DEVELOPMENT: *The act of developing. The state of being developed. A significant event, occurrence, or change. Determination of the best techniques for applying a new device or process to production of goods or services. As in music: Elaboration of a theme with rhythmic and harmonic variations. The central section of a movement in sonata form, in which the theme is elaborated and explored.*

PROCESS: *A series of actions, changes, or functions bringing about a result: the process of digestion; A series of operations performed in the making or treatment of a product: a manufacturing process; leather dyed during the tanning process. Progress; passage: the process of time; events now in process.*

DEVELOPMENT PROCESS: *Hell*

Most people in the motion picture industry know what development is, but few truly understand the process of development. Most hate it, as it can be long and arduous—years and years may go by, drafts replace other drafts of the same screenplay, writers come and go; talent is attached, falls out, and is then re-attached; projects get placed into turnaround, languish for years, get picked up again and fast-tracked, and, sometimes—if you're lucky—your project is developed to the point where it gets the coveted greenlight. That is what every producer, director, writer, or development executive hopes for—to see the movie they've labored over for years become a reality on celluloid. Over 80 percent of the scripts in development at the studios are waiting to see the light of day. So how does this all work? How does it begin, this elusive process, this journey into development hell—a term used often by producers and writers to explain the lengthy amount of time it takes to get a movie produced—where does it all begin? Back in the late eighties and early nineties, a number of scripts were sold for a million dollars (thus starting the million-dollar spec sale bandwagon). Among them was *The Ticking Man*, by Brian Helgeland and Manny Coto, which was submitted to the studios with a ticking clock in 1990. The clock's still ticking, the film *still* hasn't been made! *The Cheese Stands Alone*, by Kathy McWorter, also sold for a million dollars and had the auspicious footnote of being the first million-dollar spec for a comedy, let alone for a female writer. Lastly, Lee and Janet Batchelor's *Smoke & Mirrors* followed suit as another million dollar spec. There are countless others that have not made it to the theatre, although *Smoke & Mirrors* has been periodically listed in pre-production for years. It must be hell to have a high profile script deal and ten or fifteen years later, still no movie credit. However, hell can be filled with pleasure as well as pain—mothers explain birthing a child as the most painful and yet most wonderful experience they've ever had. Birthing a screenplay and getting a movie made is equally painful, equally powerful, and both miraculous in the end.

It all begins with an idea, an article, a book, a true story, and/or a screenplay. Sound easy? Well, once you identify the story you want to sell, what do you do with it? Who do you go to? What happens to it once it's in the Hollywood system? Who are the players involved? How can you help the process along? Exploring the different facets of the development process and the people involved will help you get a better handle on how to maneuver your project through Hollywood. It takes a lot of time, a lot of tenacity, and no small degree of perseverance, but in the end, there can be great satisfaction knowing you collaborated with others to make a great movie.

WHAT HAPPENS TO A SCREENPLAY
When It Is Submitted To A Studio

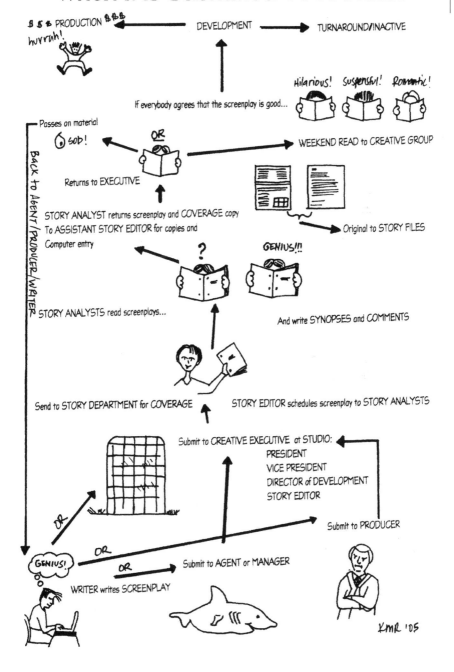

KMR '05

So, if that's the case, why does everyone complain about the movies being made in Hollywood? You have so many people working together to get it right, how can there be so many turkeys?

No one starts out wanting to make a bad movie. However, there are so many movies released each year, which means that they all can't be A+ fare, though quite a high percentage are good and some are actually quite brilliant. There are also many kinds of movies: specialty films, art house films, or independent films (those that have limited releases but are strong character-driven stories), high concept films (concept driven—does it have a hook to it that can be described in one line?), action/adventure, horror or thriller, romantic comedy, sci-fi or fantasy, western, musical, docudrama...and the list goes on.

With so many varieties of genre, sometimes Hollywood panders to the commercial aspect, sometimes to the highbrow film. Sometimes a film is just a programmer (a movie that has a target audience and fills a void for their release schedule). Other times, it's a tentpole release (a movie that's anchored to the seasonal schedule and intended to be a blockbuster, i.e., *The Day After Tomorrow* [2004], *Pirates of the Caribbean* [2003], *Harry Potter* [2001-2011], *The Lord of the Rings Trilogy* [2001-2003], *Spider-man* [2002 and 2004 so far] to name a few). No matter what kind of movie is made, it has been treated with a lot of consideration and care through what is known as the development process in an effort to make it the best product the studio and/or independent filmmaker can produce. Sometimes it works, sometimes it doesn't, but the one thing that remains clear is the intention to entertain an audience with a compelling, enlightening, shocking, amusing, or enjoyable story. Maybe the story takes you on a journey to a place you've never been. Maybe the story is more accessible and identifiable to an audience—something that we've all experienced or gone through. Or, maybe we laugh or cry at a story that mirrors our own successes, failures, or flaws. Development gives the opportunity to flesh out all the nuances and layers of our humanity to make a cohesive tale that an audience might respond to and embrace.

It is a necessary evil where many professionals add their two cents worth of suggestions in order to:

- Make a story better and stronger.
- Dig deeper into characters so that their arcs or journeys truly go from Point A to Point B determining the growth of that character (we like to call this "peeling the onion").

- Heighten the *turning points* in a story, which might surprise the audience and thereby make the story less predictable.
- Execute a story in a way we haven't seen before.
- Entertain or enlighten an audience.
- Shed light on a subject matter in order to provoke a response.

These are the goals of most producers and development executives.

It's a known fact that most writers feel that the latest draft of their screenplay is the best. It's ready to go out into the world and be made. Ask any writer and they will tell you horror stories of what happened to their screenplay as it went through the development process at a studio and how it was perfect before *those people* got their hands on the project. It's an equally well-known fact that most of the time the screenplay is *not* ready to be shot. There's still a lot of work to be done to bring the script up to a level that warrants a studio writing a hefty check for its production.

Enter the development executive. When the project is bought by a studio and the final round of development notes are given to the writer, the development executive might be viewed as the villain—but in essence, if writers and producers would realize that the development executive wants to get the movie made just as much as they do, then they might be able to view the process as less adversarial and consider the executive as a champion of their work and on their team. And who is the team? It takes many people to write, sell, develop, and eventually produce a story on film. Who are they? What do they actually do? How do they all fit into this process? When and where did it all begin?

To understand the creative process, you have to look at the beginning of film, when motion pictures were in their infancy and history was being made.

The creative process doesn't stop after you've written a script. In Hollywood, it just begins!

MAN OF 1,000 FACES   MAN OF 1,000 I.D.'s

2

"From Photoplay to Screenplay"
a brief history of story film

The history of the "story film," the "picture play," or the "photoplay," as they were commonly called in the early part of the twentieth century, is a compelling one. It might be surprising to find that our interest in moving pictures dates back to the 1600s. A contraption known as The Magic Lantern was the forerunner to the motion picture or slide projector. It had pictures painted on glass and the glass was placed in front of a lantern in a dark room. "Magically," those pictures would appear on an opposite wall, sometimes using dissolves and effects to create motion. Thus began man's fascination of mixing motion with photographic theories. Another forerunner to the motion picture projector was the Zoetrope. Invented in 1834 by William George Horner, it consisted of a drum which contained a set of still images (not unlike a film strip) that turned in a circular fashion, creating the illusion of motion. However, it wasn't until Leland

Stanford, railroad magnate and former Governor of California, hired a photographer named Eadweard Muybridge on an impulsive whim that movement was actually captured and portrayed on film. Stanford wanted to prove that when racehorses galloped, they lifted all four feet from the ground. With a shutter mechanism designed by a seventeen-year-old engineer named John Isaacs, Muybridge placed several cameras in a row, keeping the shutters open, and connected them all to a device that was triggered only when the horses galloped by. In 1882, a kind of "flipbook" was put together with the photos capturing the movement of the horse's legs. Stanford was right; horses do lift all four of their legs when they gallop.

Not long after, Thomas Alva Edison invented the kinetoscope, a cabinet holding fifty feet of celluloid that revolved on spools, with a peephole window for the film to be viewed by an individual. The word "kinetoscope" originated from the Greek words "kineto" meaning "movement" and "scopos" meaning "to watch." Edison compared the kinetoscope to one of his other inventions, the phonograph, saying it's "an instrument which does for the *eye* what the phonograph does for the *ear*." The year was 1888.

Edison's Kinetoscope circa 1891

THE SILENT ERA

Motion pictures would become a successful industry in less than a decade, with single-viewer kinetoscopes giving way to films projected for mass audiences in what were originally known as Nickelodeons, which then gave way to larger and more ornate movie palaces. On May 21, 1895, a four-minute prizefight by Otway Latham had the honor of being the first public exhibition or screening of a motion picture. At first, the films were records of historic events—for example, the funeral for William McKinley in 1901 was a forerunner to the modern day newsreel. Other films had acrobats or dancers. In 1903, the first storytelling picture, *The Great Train Robbery*, changed the face of motion pictures forever. Produced by Edison Studios and written and directed by Edwin S. Porter, the idea for a narrative film was born and with it more movie theatres to exhibit the films, thus creating a huge demand for moving pictures with plots. This demand made way for a new occupation—that of the story scenarist or scenario editor, a forerunner to the reader/story analyst or story editor of today.

Around this same period, Biograph Pictures built the first motion picture studio in the world to rely on artificial light, beating out Thomas Edison for that title. This allowed the filmmaker to control conditions inside a sound stage without having to go on location. Foreseeing the future, Biograph opened a Los Angeles office in 1906 and two years later, the legendary filmmaker, D.W. Griffith, became its star director.

Biograph was also the first studio to shift their focus to fictional "feature-length" films. The word *feature* became the vernacular for story films, or photoplays, and pertained to any multi-reel film of two to eight reels. These multi-reel feature films began distribution after 1910. Meanwhile, Colonel William Selig, George K. Spoor, and Sigmond Lubin of Chicago started manufacturing movie equipment and producing films on their own. In France, the Lumiere Freres, Gaumont, Pathe-Freres, and Meles started producing films; in England, Charles Urban started the Warwick Company. Film was a business and it was growing by leaps and bounds. It was a business with no boundaries or limitations except that of the patent for the projection equipment.

As more and more producers appeared on the scene, Edison scrambled to protect his patent of the kinetoscope (the motion picture viewer) as well as the kinetograph (the actual camera) and his lawyers took many of the producers in the New York area to court, causing them to flee to other parts of the country to escape Edison's hounds and still continue to produce films just one step ahead of Edison's private detectives.

Between 1908-1910, Los Angeles proved to be the haven in which many moviemakers sought refuge. It was William Selig, known for producing "Fatty" Arbuckle comedies, cowboy films, and animal movies, who discovered the city. While Edison's lawyers pursued these "outlaw" filmmakers for infringing on his patent, Selig and Spoor were the last to be attacked—mainly because they were in Chicago and out of Edison's reach. Then, they headed out west to do cowboy films where the dry climate reduced their outlay of money. Choosing Los Angeles also had another advantage—it was close to the Mexican border. With a lookout planted nearby, if strangers happened to appear on or near the set, one signal from the lookout was enough to quit work that day and hustle the very expensive and very rare cameras and equipment into a motorcar (also a new invention at the time) and dash across the border into Mexico. After producing the narrative film, *The Count of Monte Cristo* (1908) on the west coast, Selig firmly planted his base of operations in Los Angeles. Thus, his Polyscope Film Co., originally based in Chicago, would become Selig-Polyscope circa 1909 in L.A.

Within a year, L.A. was bustling with film folk. The Los Angeles locals didn't care about lawsuits or copyright infringements. By 1912, the Federal courts ruled against Edison in a lawsuit brought on by William Fox. It became a victory for the independents (hard to believe that Fox was considered an indie at one time). Interestingly enough, both Biograph and Edison went out of business around that same time because of the increasing number of production companies and competition, thus paving the way for a brand new movie mogul and studio system.

PHOTOPLAYS BECOME FEATURE FILMS

With well-funded studios such as MGM, Paramount, Warner Bros., First National, and Fox popping up all over Los Angeles, and smaller studios at that time, like United Artists and Universal Pictures, the business of making films began to take shape. While these studios answered to the money people in New York, the West Coast operations were strictly about production.

Paramount's Adolph Zukor, W. W. Hodkinson, and Jesse Lasky, were considered the most important architects of the Hollywood system. Introducing a new method for feature production distribution, causing the others to follow, they raised their exhibitor rental rates from $500-$700 a week (compared to another studio's rate of $100-$150 a week). Gross movie rentals increased to an extraordinary fee in its time: $100,000 to $125,000 per picture, and with it the need for production to increase from two features a week to three and four pictures. Audiences were restless for more stories and exhibitors couldn't supply the public with enough of this newfound entertainment.

To keep up with demand, the studios hired more people to read all the submissions and also to generate their own stories. Story departments and story editors were created—though they were originally called scenario departments and scenario editors—and studios began to sift through Broadway plays, short stories, manuscripts, and magazine articles to find material to turn into film. With all these submissions came a need to establish a system that would archive the submissions with some sort of synopsis; a record that would prevent the countless lawsuits that would soon follow. Everyone wanted their ideas made into films. Everyone thought Hollywood was stealing *their* ideas, even back then! A system had to be put in place to prove who submitted what to whom, and when.

Writing for film was brand new. It did not rely on any established literary forms such as novels or plays but rather was about plot and visuals. Ideas poured in from all over the country. At first, the studios didn't even pay for them; they then began paying a nominal amount, e.g., a hundred dollars a story. A scenario editor's job was to transfer the story into a useable shooting script also called a continuity script.

One of the first story scenarists was Frank E. Woods, who is considered to have written the first feature-length motion picture scenario, and who oversaw Biograph's story department where he became filmmaking pioneer D.W. Griffith's right hand man. With Griffith, Woods wrote some of the most influential films of their time, including *The Birth of a Nation* (1915) which was based upon a stageplay Woods discovered called "The Klansman." He, more than any other person, influenced the structure of the photoplay, or screenplay, as we know it today. Not only that, Woods is credited with innovating methods of production—including writers meetings and implementing supervisors in charge of production units. Woods was probably the forerunner of the development and production executives in Hollywood today.

A NEW BUSINESS REQUIRES NEW MATERIAL

In those early days, writers were under contract to studios. It was a writer's job to find material and ideas for films, as some story editors still do today; the difference being that then writers would take the story or idea and actually rewrite it into a shooting script. Sometimes they would originate an idea and translate it for the screen. Since they were under contract, they didn't get those million dollar spec deals we see nowadays, and instead received a weekly paycheck. Story editors today manage readers and story departments, some read new material and suggest the studio either buy it or pass on it. They do not rewrite ideas or ready them into any semblance of a movie. What was once a very creative role has become more and more administrative.

Along with the onslaught of plot-driven films, there were many books, as well as articles in magazines, written on how to write a photoplay and how to submit stories and ideas to a studio. It's remarkable that a lot of what was written then, still applies to the motion picture industry today. It is fascinating to read these early "how to" books on an industry that was so young, and realize the same commentary still applies for today's writers.

Considered to be the first screenwriting book of its kind, circa 1911, *Picture Plays and How to Write Them* by E.J. Muddle (late editor of *The Bioscope* magazine) offers a dated yet interesting, humorous view, proving the point that not every screenwriting book offers good sound advice:

- "Whilst producers complain continually of the lack of fresh, strong plots, would-be writers cry equally bitterly that the difficulty is not to write plays, but to sell them!"
- "What we require are good, strong plots and rapid action, depicted in a way easily understood by audiences."
- "When you have ascertained the main theme, put down the characters in the order of their importance to the story. The hero and the heroine, the villain, the fool who unwittingly saves the situation, and the subsidiary characters who help to round off the story."
- "Therefore, when writing your own scenarios, remember the Golden Rule: Be as simple and as brief as possible. Cut out every character who hampers the plot, but make quite sure before you do so that the character is not superfluous."
- "Everyone knows that all dramas can be divided into three main parts: the beginning, the middle, and the end. In the drama the three parts must bear their proper relationship one to the other. They must be strung together so that one part leads directly to the next. The interest in this sequence of events must not be interrupted by the intrusion of extraneous incidents which have no place in the story."
- "The fewer the characters the better. The first scene should grip the interest at once. Fail to do that, and your scenario stands a very good chance of not being interesting at all. Too much stress cannot be laid upon the first scene."
- "Don't have impossible situations or unnatural ones. Be true to life all the time. If you have to force a situation, or make a character do something unnatural, then your play is not as good as it should be."

THE PROCESS OF SUBMISSIONS IN THE EARLY 1900s

Surprisingly, the studios were receiving over 500,000 submissions annually and from those, less than 1 percent were accepted. The rest were returned to their writers, provided the submission had been accompanied by return postage. Sound familiar? However, studios would advertise in *Variety* and magazines, soliciting material from would-be writers in order to fill their pipeline of production.

Writers submitting stories or synopses to the studios were called contributors. These stories and ideas would go directly to the scenario editor who might hand it over to his or her assistant to read. If the reader liked the idea, he or she would pass it back to the editor to take a look at and possibly develop it further, or make changes to it to satisfy the studio and its needs. After turning it into a working script or continuity script, the scenario editor would then assign it to a producing director for production. The director would then cast the movie with members of the stock company that worked under contract to the studio, and prepare the scenes with costumes, props, and scenery. The scenario editor was in charge of the script until it passed into the director's hands. The scenario editor and director were the ones to decide whether a story merited production or not. Some studios also had scenario editors in charge of productions.

By 1912, the American Copyright Law was officially amended to recognize motion pictures so that features and shorts were at last perceived to be the products of authors, rather than stories that just happened to be made up by the actors on the screen. The studios had to register their films with the Copyright Office at the Library of Congress in Washington D.C. Approximately 25,000 films were registered between 1911 and 1929. Since they were all silent films, the material registered were scenarios or synopses—what we might call a treatment today.

Forty million Americans were going to the movie theatres by 1920, prompting the twenty major studios at that time to race to produce enough product to satisfy the marketplace. Creative talents D.W. Griffith, Charlie Chaplin, Mary Pickford, and Douglas Fairbanks, in an effort to have more control over their work, joined together to form United Artists, causing Chaplin to exclaim, "The inmates have taken over the asylum." Fox grew from a tiny small-framed cottage on Western and Sunset Boulevard to a lot able to accommodate twenty productions shooting simultaneously while Warner Bros. attributed their growth to the likes of John Barrymore, Busby Berkeley, and Al Jolson. By the mid 1920s, these studios resembled small serfdoms—in which each had a despot and, below them, all the workers building the fantasy known as Hollywood.

WHAT'S WRONG WITH YOUR PHOTOPLAY STORY?
Some hints to the amateur who cannot understand why his photoplays are rejected

by Jerome Lachenbruch
Published by FILM PLAY Magazine, June 1922

1) Don't write your manuscript in pencil—Have it typewritten. Your predecessors have made the readers take to wearing glasses.

2) Don't point out the excellence of your script. The reader has had years of experience and has read thousands of stories before yours came to his desk. Give him credit for a little perspicacity and judgment.

3) Don't write a scenario. This is the technical form in which a story is cast for the director. Specialists in the form of writing take your synopsis and arrange it into scenes. A scene usually changes whenever the position of the camera must be shifted. Only a man who has worked in a studio may be expected to know this.

4) Don't write your story in 100 words. Make it from 1,000-3,000 words, and in your eagerness to talk about the story, don't forget to tell it.

5) Don't forget that a single idea isn't a story.

6) Don't delude yourself into thinking that a photoplay company is waiting for your particular manuscript and is interested in your ideas. A letter to the effect that you have some good ideas may be very interesting, but the picture companies haven't any time to bother with your ideas. They've been fooled too often that way. Now you've got to suffer for the thousands of times that your literary ancestors have cried: "Wolf!" Get your ideas into story form and send them in.

7) Don't try to hold up a company. Be satisfied to have your story accepted. Terms can be arranged later.

8) Don't ever get the idea in your head that a motion picture producer is waiting to steal your story. Did you even stop to think that it would be cheaper to pay you several thousand dollars for a story than to have you bring suit for the theft of your effusion? Remember that the photoplay producer knows the damning voice of unsavory publicity.

9) Don't think that your story is worth more than one by Rupert Hughes or Mary Roberts Rinehart. Be modest.
10) Don't write a line until you have learned to express your ideas in untrimmed English.

To these few precepts should be added a word of advice to the effect that would-be photo-playwrights should read more widely, see more photoplays, and discover for themselves how rich a literature has already been translated into the language of the screen. Originality is not, as some have maintained, a gift that a few have and the rest of us have not. It's knowing what has already been done and then not doing it again. There may be a limited number of fundamental plot situations, but they permit inexhaustible variations. The more one reads, the less presumptuous one becomes and the less eager to shout about one's genius. There are still millions of original stories left in the world. Surely the reader can find one.

THE PIONEERS OF STORY FILMS

While trying to track down the origins of many of the procedures used in today's story departments, there are a number of pioneers who kept cropping up in our brief history of film.

It is interesting to note that women played an enormous part in the early days of film—many of them worked at the studios as readers and scenario/story editors; many of them wrote classic films. Frances Marion wrote for Mary Pickford while June Mathis wrote for Valentino, and Anita Loos wrote for Douglas Fairbanks. A number of these women also wrote books or pamphlets on how to write for the movies expressing the same emphasis on story and characters as is still taught in film schools around the world. Sure, there were male scenario editors, too, but D.W. Griffith, truly the first 'star' director, believed that "if women didn't like a movie, it would be a failure and if they liked it, it would be a success." What a far cry from today's world where the target audience is the 18-34 white male! The women were important contributors during the first thirty years of the movie biz, writing such films as *Blood And Sand* (1921), *Greed* (1924), *The Champ* (1931), *Dinner at Eight* (1933), *San Francisco* (1936), and *The Women* (1939). From 1912-1939, women working as scenario editors and screenwriters had a great influence on the stories the studios made into film.

With the 1920s, the industry had standardized the process into a more streamlined system. By 1921, each studio employed a scenario editor. Movies were first conceived, written up in a visual synopsis, and prepared for shooting, physically shot, then edited into a finished product which was sold or rented out to *exhibitors* (theatre owners—another booming business) and marketed to the public.

THE EARLY SCENARIO WRITERS

These early pioneers of story were the ones who laid down the tracks for what we now know as the development process. In an industry still in its infancy, they helped shape the story department and the development systems that are still in effect today.

Frank E. Woods—Became D.W. Griffith's right hand scenario editor beginning at Biograph in 1911, and later at Mutual Films. In 1917, he joined Famous Players-Lasky Corporation, now Paramount Pictures. He is credited with writing the first full-length picture scenario and was one of the founders of the Academy of Motion Picture Arts and Sciences and the Screen Writers Guild (SWG) now known as the Writers Guild of America (WGA).

Epes Winthrop Sargent—Originally a staff writer for *Variety* and managing editor of Moving Picture World. Along with Frank E. Woods, was known as one of the early pioneers of the photoplay. His book, *The Techniques of The Photoplay*, published in 1913, is still quoted today.

Captain Leslie T. Peacocke—One of the world's foremost writers and scenario editors, he started at Universal Pictures and went on to work for World Film Corp. in 1914. He published a book in 1916 of a collection of his articles from *Photoplay* magazine titled *Hints on Photoplay Writing*. His no-nonsense approach to writing the photoplay is still relevant today.

Anita Loos—The story goes that at age thirteen she sold a story, *The New York Hat* (1912), to D.W. Griffith for $25.00. However, it is debatable whether she was that young. Signed by Griffith as a scenarist when she was barely twenty, she contributed to writing *Intolerance* (1916) along with Frank E. Woods and D.W. Griffith. She also wrote books with her writer/director husband, John Emerson: *How to Write Photoplays* in 1920, and *Breaking into the Movies* in 1921. From there, she went to work with many of Hollywood's leading stars and wrote 105 films in both the silent and talking era.

June Mathis—Though her life was short, she wrote 104 movies from 1916 to her death in 1927, working only in the silent era. With Rudolph Valentino as her star, she wrote such legendary silents as *Blood and Sand* (1922), *Camille* (1921), and *The Four Horsemen of the Apocalypse* (1921) as well as Erich Von Stroheim's *Greed* (1924).

Frances Marion—Her career crossed over from silent to sound with many of the great films of that era including *The Champ* (1931), *Camille* (1936), and *Anna Christie* (1931). Her long-time relationship with Mary Pickford resulted in some of the best movies of Pickford's career. From 1915-1954, she wrote in excess of 160 films with two remakes of her earlier films (*The Champ* and *Dinner at Eight*) made posthumously in 1979 and 1989 respectively. Her book, *How to Write Film Stories*, is truly one of the forerunners of today's books on screenwriting. Long considered one of the great architects of the talkies, she was by far one of the most powerful screenwriters in Hollywood, commanding $17,000 per week at the height of her career.

Sam Marx—A chance meeting with Irving Thalberg (then head of production at MGM) resulted in Marx moving to Hollywood to become story editor for MGM in the early 1930s. There, he supervised a group of writers that included some of the great literary giants of our time— including William Faulkner, Dorothy Parker, and F. Scott Fitzgerald. He became a producer and then a full-time writer in his later years.

WHAT THEY SAID THEN...

On Loglines

"If you cannot state the gist of a play in three lines, it lacks backbone."
—*Frances Marion (1937)*

The Punch

"It may be that someone will presently find a more expressive term than "punch" for that quality of the story that lifts it from the commonplace. Punch possesses a variety of synonyms—heart interest, grip, suspense. It is what makes a story but if it's left out it's the motorboat without a motor, the gun without the powder."
—*Epes Winthrop Sargent (1913)*

On Plot
"Crisis and Conflict are the great essentials of a dramatic story. Something must happen and happen speedily. There must be conflict between opposing elements.

—Anita Loos/John Emerson (1920)

"An illogical plot is an imposition, and impositions are boomerangs."

—Captain Leslie T. Peacock (1916)

On the Climax
"It is a wise writer who knows when his climax is reached. When the end follows your climax it means that there is some sort of suspense still unresolved. Too much action coming after your climax weakens the supreme moment of denouement."

—Louella Parsons (1915)

On Character
"VERY frequently someone tells me, 'I have a wonderful plot for a movie!' I always am impelled to respond, 'But have you interesting characters?'"

—Frances Marion (1937)

"A man of distinctly unpleasant character may have an attractive personality; the wolf may wear sheep's clothing. Personality includes mannerisms, superficial conduct and appearance, while character refers to the nature and quality of the individual."

—Frances Marion (1937)

On Structure
"There must be logical obstacles—as poverty, war or destiny—which prevent the characters from achieving their will—in the "big scene" they either conquer those obstacles or are conquered."

—Anita Loos/John Emerson (1920)

On Finding Ideas
"A very real and instinctive interest in your fellow men is a prime necessity. The knowledge of life that is most useful to the writer is that which he gains by observing and understanding the motives and acts of other people."

—Frances Marion (1937)

"Your local motion picture theatre is indeed your greatest "tool." Attend regularly, see as many as possible and think about them afterwards. Try to analyze them and get the author's point of view. Try to realize what it was that sold those stories. Become familiar with the current stars and directors."

—Anita Loos/John Emerson (1920)

On Marketability

"Each story should have an idea in it greater than merely an interesting series of events. It should have a central thought or purpose, not necessarily heavy. I do not think the public likes to think that it is being preached to, or obviously taught; these elements in a story should be incidental."

—Frank Woods (1916)

"The exhibitor wants the sort of story that can be exploited from the box office point of view, for a photoplay that does not lend itself to advertising and publicity in all forms will not draw the crowd."

—Anita Loos/John Emerson (1920)

THE TALKIES GIVE SCREENPLAYS THEIR VOICE

The studios were firmly established in Hollywood by 1925, and the film business, although still in its infancy, was a booming export. While this new industry was refining the production-distribution-exhibition formula, it was also fine-tuning the process of storytelling. In 1927, the next technological boom hit Hollywood and changed the face of entertainment forever—something that was so momentous that it paved the way for other technologies in the 20th Century. *Talking* pictures! What a novelty! Warner Bros.' *The Jazz Singer*, starring Al Jolson, gave the studios a whole new business. Now, they were able to really tell stories and, now, we could hear them. Sound changed everything about the film business. Actors came in droves from the New York stage, while many popular silent actors, such as handsome leading man John Gilbert, couldn't make the grade. Voice and projection suddenly mattered to audiences—and therefore, to careers. *Singing in the Rain*, the 1952 MGM musical, delightfully conveys the silent star's transition, or lack thereof, to talking pictures.

It wasn't long before silents became talkies, bringing with it a whole new way of writing and developing screenplays...dialogue! Now it wasn't enough to have visuals and simplistic plots, now the actors had to talk. Scenario writers, instead of using visuals to tell stories, now had to write full screenplays. The studios employed staffs of screenwriters to adapt plays, historical sagas, and novels, as well as original ideas. By the 1930s, the studios drafted such novelists as William Faulkner, F. Scott Fitzgerald, Dorothy Parker, Ben Hecht and Charles MacArthur, Moss Hart, and John Steinbeck, just to name a few, to come to Hollywood and write motion pictures. Story editing took on a new form. No longer did they write all the movies for the studios, now story editors oversaw the development of projects by other writers. They would write comments and make suggestions on behalf of the studio and were truly the forerunner of the development execs today. Synopses turned into what we know as "coverage," and a "comments" section evaluated by the reader/story analyst on the merits of the screenplay and its progress was added later. One of the more famous story editors of the thirties was Samuel Marx, who oversaw a huge slate of films for MGM including *The Thin Man* (1934), *Goodbye Mr. Chips* (1939), and *Mutiny on the Bounty* (1935), as well as supervised the illustrious stable of writers mentioned above. The thirties also brought with it a huge change in the industry—for now it was a true working business. No longer run by the founders, but by high paid "suits"—executives who kept a tight reign on costs to keep the studios stable and profitable. It was also a time when studios defined themselves with distinctive styles, i.e., Universal was known for horror films, MGM had "more stars than in heaven," and so on. The studios maintained story departments in Los Angeles, New York, and London where they scoured the publishing houses and theatres for new material. Scouts were employed to secure material before it was even printed. David O. Selznick acquired the rights to *Gone with the Wind* (1939) before it was ever published. Even today, producers such as Scott Rudin use literary scouts and are notorious for taking manuscripts off the market long before their publication dates.

CONCLUSION

We've come a long way from the silents of the early twentieth century...or have we? Today, young filmmakers are making short films while studios and production companies look for many of the same basic ideas that have always attracted Hollywood—strong heroes, obstacles to overcome, characters audiences can identify with.

Today's Hollywood, much like yesteryear's, concerns itself with the telling of compelling, often times hard-hitting, yet entertaining tales that have wide audience appeal. There are more choices today and somehow it is harder than ever to identify these stories. In the beginning, every story was new. Hollywood's challenge today is to uncover original stories while executing them in a discerning way, thereby keeping the genres fresh and still appealing to a modern day audience.

John Emerson and Anita Loos evaluate script submissions.

THE 2 KINDS of HOLLYWOOD PROJECTS

the kind that
don't go anywhere

the kind that
go nowhere

3

"Every Picture Tells a Story... At Least, We Hope So!"

the story department

If you know anything about the industry, then you've heard of the infamous "Story Department." This department exists at all the major studios. It also exists at some "mini-majors"—smaller, fully or partially financed studios, which may have a distribution deal with the major studios. Production companies, literary agencies such as William Morris, ICM, and CAA, TV networks, and cable television networks all rely on their story departments. Some have full story departments, others rely on a database of coverage done by assistants or freelance readers. Why? Well, for one thing, it gives them a log of all scripts and stories entering their hallowed halls. Another reason is that it protects them legally from plagiarism. It also helps save time when a screenplay is covered (material read by readers who then write a synopsis and comment) so executives can decide whether to take the time to read the whole script or realize after reading the synopsis and comment (commonly called coverage), that the project isn't right for them. Rest assured that someone is reading your material, synopsizing it, and commenting on its merit before deciding whether to bump it upstairs or pass on it, then and there. And lastly, it is a great library and therefore a great resource for executives to find new writers, seek out old material in their archives, and find new material. This department is the hub of the motion picture division with a vast database of information. It is the foundation for every studio. And while Hollywood is always changing, the path a screenplay takes remains the same. However, the title and function of a story editor at a studio has changed considerably since its origins. Today's story editor usually runs the whole story department, managing the day-to-day work of assigning story analysts to read scripts submitted to the studio by the many producers, production companies, agents, writers, directors, and entertainment lawyers in town. They also maintain the smooth running of the story department, prepare the studio status and development reports for the studio executives, and act as the liaison between the creative executive staff and the story department.

One of the main functions of the story department is to be responsible for maintaining legal records of all material submitted to the studio (i.e., screenplays, books, manuscripts, stageplays, short stories, comic books, magazine and newspaper articles, remakes of foreign films, songs, and treatments), which is to say, any story that might make a potential movie. These materials are called submissions. The story department oversees the studio's archives of all the submissions and projects in development as well as produced and unproduced projects in the studio's library.

THE STORY ANALYST OR READER

With a weekly flow of approximately 60 to 110 submissions sent to creative executives at the studios (compared to a production company receiving ten to twenty-five submissions each week), the executives send these submissions to the story department who then organize the material to be logged in and assigned to a story analyst, the official union term for a studio reader. In 1999, the Story Analysts Union (Local 854) merged with the Editors Union (Local 700), which is part of *IATSE* (International Alliance for Theatrical Stage Employees). While the major studios only use union readers, production companies and literary agencies use non-union readers. This is because the studios agreed to sign a *Basic Agreement* with the Story Analysts Union to only use their members. Production companies and literary agencies do not have this agreement. The studios generally have eight to twelve readers on staff. A production company may have one staff reader and a few freelance readers. Many studio readers have read for the same company for ten years or more.

Though it is difficult to become a member, some readers are able to join the union when the union roster is low and/or by working the "graveyard" shift, which means reading scripts over night. It's one way a studio can cutback on overtime. Union readers can make up to $35.00+ an hour and work a 40-hour week. They read one and a half to two screenplays a day, cover-to-cover, which comes out to about eight to ten scripts a week, or 350 pieces of coverage a year. Out of all the material submitted to one reader in a week's time, maybe one out of ten scripts are considered for development (approximately thirty scripts a year, per reader) and just because it gets a "consider" doesn't mean it will be bought by the studio. But it will get flagged and read by an executive. Non-union freelance readers, however, have more flexible hours and usually earn around $40 to $85 per script. The work is the same; the money slightly less. It usually takes between four to six hours to read and evaluate one screenplay.

What exactly does a story analyst do? They read! And they read and they read! Then they write, they write, and they write! They must accurately convey the story in a one and a half to two-page synopsis and make intelligent, objective evaluations on material submitted to the company for consideration in a one-page comment; why they liked it or didn't like it, and possibly provide a few suggestions on how to improve it. Excellent writing skills, understanding the structure of a story, and possessing the ability to make concrete suggestions on what elements are missing in a story, are a reader's strengths. In addition to writing coverage, they also write:

- *Comparison Coverage*—using a previous draft's synopsis, the reader compares the latest draft and lists the changes.
- *Writing Samples*—the screenplay itself is not submitted to the studio for consideration, but the writer is possibly up for a specific open writing assignment or maybe submitted in general as an introduction to the writer. Even on spec coverage, the writer might be flagged with a "consider writer."
- *Scene Breakdowns*—usually done for projects already in development at the studio, each scene of the screenplay is described in a sentence with its corresponding page number.
- *Legal Comparisons*—comparing different screenplays with different authors to ascertain similarities for possible lawsuits.

- *Project Development Notes*—outlining problems and issues that need to be worked on while offering suggestions for the rewrite of projects already in development.
- *Page-by-Page Breakdown*—similar to Scene Breakdowns but instead compares two different drafts of a screenplay already in development, listing the page-by-page changes.

To become a reader, it is best to send a kick-ass query letter along with three sample coverages—using a novel and two screenplays—to the story editor. There are many courses offered at UCLA Extension, American Film Institute, and USC, as well as countless other film schools and organizations, that teach the art of writing coverage. The United Talent Agency (UTA) job list is also a great resource for finding jobs as a reader. This list is forwarded via email from one person to the next. The problem is, you have to know someone who has access to it and get on their distribution list, either directly from the agency or from someone else who receives it. It's like a game of "hot potato," it's passed around the 'net' begetting more and more circulation. All you need is one person who receives it and ask them to forward it to you.

The reader position is usually a stepping-stone to becoming a development executive. The average professional union reader with years of experience is approximately 40+ years old and earns an average of $73,000 a year, including health benefits and company perks. Some union readers make more than their story editor bosses or even the development executives. But one thing is for certain, the fate of literary material lies in the hands of these readers.

Most readers either have been or want to be screenwriters. In the movie *Sunset Boulevard* (1950), the character of Betty Schaefer was a reader in the script department at Paramount Pictures. At the beginning of the movie, she exclaims to Joe, "I don't want to be a reader all my life! I want to *write*." Art imitating life or is it life imitating art?

THE STORY EDITOR OR EXECUTIVE STORY EDITOR

The story department may have a few assistants along with a staff of story analysts who report to a story editor or Executive Story Editor, who oversees the department. In some cases, a story editor might be promoted to Vice President of the Story Department. They are all part of the "creative group" and are under contract as part of the management team to the studio. The story editor carries out executive policy decisions and supports activities requested by creative executives and executives in various departments within the studio such as Business Affairs, Legal Affairs, Physical Production, Marketing, Television and Film Acquisition. They also attend regular creative group staff meetings such as the weekend read meetings and the weekly business affairs meeting, all the while jotting down new information to be included in the studio status reports. Aside from supervising and maintaining the story department and its library, some story editors provide development status reports, weekly "consider" coverage reports, "talent to pursue" reports, and oversee the preparation of the weekend read for the executives. They handle all personnel and employment decisions in the story department for their readers and support staff.

Usually promoted from the ranks of an assistant story editor or story department assistant, a story editor must have the ability to recognize and appreciate good writing, be highly organized, detail-oriented, computer-literate, have the ability to handle lots of pressure, and have familiarity with agent's, writer's, director's, and producer's credits. A mental database of credits can go a long way.

It is also the story editor's responsibility to evaluate readers' coverage on a regular basis and to maintain the quality of that coverage. They know the strengths and weaknesses of their individual readers. What happens if a reader and an executive disagree on the potential of a submission? The story editor might give it a read or reassign the material to a different reader.

A creative story editor and/or vice president of the story department is known to read a pile of screenplays over the weekend, maintain relationships with literary agents and managers, network with their counterparts at other studios, agencies, and production companies, help a vice president supervise projects in active development when requested, and may provide development notes to help guide the development of a project as it progresses towards production. They can initiate and participate in meetings with new writers, directors, or producers who pitch story ideas for development, evaluate student short films, attend film festivals and screenwriting competitions looking for potential creative talent, and provide suggestions of writers and directors for development projects.

THE ASSISTANT STORY EDITOR OR MANAGER OF THE STORY DEPARTMENT

Aside from assisting the story editor with various internal reports for distribution to the executives once a week, the assistant story editor also reviews the quality and accuracy of all returned coverage from the readers prior to sending it back to the executive. Their job includes prioritizing and logging in submissions from the executives, scheduling and allocating scripts and materials to readers, while maintaining the day-to-day operation of the story department computer files, consisting of coverage, projects in active development, produced and unproduced screenplays. This is where one learns a lot about who is submitting what to whom, what agents and producers are developing, and what writers are being pushed. They also carry out the daily circulation of coverage to all executives. Handling readers' office requests, assisting with computer entry of project development and status reports, and sorting the executives' submissions by priority dates are only some of the duties of the assistant story editor. They may also handle some general office management responsibilities such as invoices, office supplies, equipment, and maintenance.

OTHER STORY DEPARTMENT POSITIONS

With the merging of studios and downsizing of departments, some of these positions have been consolidated; sometimes these jobs may even overlap.

Assistant or Secretary to the Story Editor

Of course, there are the usual secretarial duties, like answering the story editor's phone or general office typing and filing, but being an assistant in the story department is like being in the trenches at the frontline. Logging in the submissions from agents, producers, and upcoming writers, arranging appointments and meetings for the story editor, assisting the story editor in possibly researching writer's and director's credits, and their representation as well as shadowing competitive development at other studios, are just the tip of the iceberg for this position. Internet database services such as Internet Movie Database and Baseline StudioSystems make this a lot easier with a few keystrokes. Two of Monika's former assistants, Erin Maher and Kay Reindl, moved off her desk, becoming story files assistants. From there, Erin was promoted to a story analyst while Kay became a story editor at a production company. Today, they are both successful television and film writers.

Story Files Assistant

Also known as a script librarian or coverage assistant, the story files assistant maintains the physical files of all coverage and all produced, unproduced, and active development screenplays the studio owns. They also log the reader's coverage into the studio database for immediate retrieval. They handle daily phone calls and pull past coverage for executives and term deal producers who request previous coverage from the studio's vast story files. They might also search the files to check for previous coverage on each submission in order to avoid duplicating a reader's previous coverage, as sometimes writers will change the title of a script or change the character names, and then resubmit the screenplay for a fresh read. The story files assistant will double-check this just in case there is pre-existing coverage from a submission a year or two ago.

Interns

Most studios use interns and have summer internship programs. The Peter Stark Producing Program at USC is well-known for supplying studios with interns and some have returned to those same studios as executives. Sometimes they work out of the story department, or for individual creative executives as well as other studio departments. Most internships are for college credit, few are paid. However, most colleges with known film programs help their students obtain internships, not only at the studios but at production companies and networks. There are a number of job lists/postings via Internet Web sites which can also be beneficial in identifying internships at various companies. Interns are a part of the Hollywood system and a good way to get your foot in the door. Rona has nurtured many interns who are working in development and writing screenplays today.

COVERAGE—IT ALL COMES DOWN TO COVERAGE!

While the backbone of the story department, coverage is the bane of existence for most writers and producers. It is a necessary evil that exists in Hollywood. But what exactly *is* coverage?

Quite simply, it's a reader's evaluation of a project (a novel, a screenplay, an article, a treatment, a comic book—anything that constitutes a story which can then be turned into a cinematic experience).

Coverage is written in present tense, recounting the "who, what, where, when, why" and tone of the story along with a one-page comment focusing on the strength and weakness of the premise, characterization, dialogue, storyline, and the writer's ability. This three or four page piece of paper can make or break a project submitted to a studio. It can also make or break a reader. There's been many a horror story about an executive passing on a project and then seeing that movie produced by another studio and become a big blockbuster hit. *Star Wars* (1977) and *Independence Day* (1996), along with many other successful films, had been passed on by one studio then successfully set up at a competing studio. And the rest is, as they say, "history!" Executives can fight for material but ultimately it ends up in the "powers-that-be" hands, who evaluate the script and/or package and make the final decision to greenlight and finance the project.

Some readers who have stuck their necks out and given coverage a "consider" or, the very rarely heard, "recommend" are promoted to creative executives. Barry Issacson was a reader at Universal Pictures and promoted to a director of development when he recommended *Field of Dreams* (1989) and moved up quickly to senior vice president of production. At that time, he also nurtured the writing talent of David Koepp, who has gone on to become one of the top writers working in the industry today. Another executive, Lenny Kornberg, was also a reader promoted to director of development and then senior vice president overseeing such movies as *River Wild* (1994), *Daylight* (1996), and *The Mummy* (1999). While a reader at Fox, he recommended the spec screenplay, *Lethal Weapon* (1987), but the studio passed and it became a blockbuster hit for Warner Bros. One studio's pass can become another studio's success. Indeed, he also recommended *Raising Arizona* (1987) while at Fox, and it did successfully get made. However, recommending or considering a project isn't enough. The executive has to garner attention from many other executives, including the president of production. All a recommendation does is flag the project, giving it additional attention. Today, Lenny and Barry are successful development executives at production companies. Carr D'Angelo was a story department assistant promoted to a reader and then upped to a director of development and, subsequently, vice president of production after making good calls on writing talent and material such as *Death Becomes Her* (1992). Currently, he is a successful producer of such films as *The Animal* (2001) and *The Hot Chick* (2002).

Ironically, coverage today follows the exact same format that was used in the 1920s and 1930s, however, those were written on onionskin paper with carbon copies attached (oh, those pre-photocopying days) to be placed in the story files.

First Page of Coverage from 1927—picture this on onionskin paper.

MAR 30 1927

STUDIO COVERAGE

TOILERS OF THE SEA

VICTOR HUGO 1866

SYNOPSIS

BY

ANONYMOUS

Mess Lethierry, of St. Sampson in the Island of Guernsey, found he was getting too old to sail a sailing vessel. To make more money for himself and his beautiful niece, Deruchette, he determined to investigate a new kind of ship that was not moved by sails, but by a strange power that came from boiling water.

He built a vessel and when the new engine came from France, he called the ship Durande and his pride in her was barely second to his worship of his niece.

When the boat was launched, the frightened people called the roaring, smoking monster the "devil-boat." But the boat being able to carry more in shorter time, became a great success. Laid up with rheumatism, Lethierry gave the command to Sieur Clubin, who had a reputation for honesty, but was only biding his time to make a good haul and put one over on the trusting fools.

A man called Rantaine stole three thousand pounds from Lethierry and tried to escape with it. Sieur Clubin, who had acquired a new invention, an American revolver, followed Rantaine to the coastwatched him kill a guard, so he might escape unnoticed. Then Clubin stepped forward and leveling his revolver at Rantaine forced him to give up the money which had been changed into three Bank of England notes. They were in a tin tobacco box. Clubin put them in his pocket and covered Rantaine with his gun until the latter had reached his boat. Rantaine calls to Clubin that he will inform Lethierry that he has paid over three thousand

```
pounds to Clubin for Lethierry, saying, I know you
are an honest man.

    But Clubin was not, and made plans to keep the
money. In spite of protestations, he takes the
DURANDE out in a fogorders Full speed ahead and the
vessel is wrecked. The passengers and crew are
taken off in the life-boat. Clubin refuses to leave
the ship. When the life-boat is off, Clubin pre-
pares to swim ashore and make his get-away, but
thru a rift in the fog, he sees that instead of
having struck the Hanway rocks, near shore, he had
hit the DOUVRES, two mighty pillars of rock, far
from shore. But he does not despairjumps off into
the water after tying the box, containing the
money, around his waist, he sinks deep and feels
himself seized by the foot.
```

Coverage helps executives make an informed decision about whether to put the material into development or pass on the material. Some companies use a "rating box" which is also referred to as "box scores" or the "grid." Marking an "x" in each box as either "excellent," "good," "fair," or "poor," they rate the premise, characterization, storyline, and dialogue.

Readers are also asked to make a recommendation on whether the company should pass on the script or pursue it as a project. Usually with rating codes of "Recommend," "Consider," or "Not Recommend," or "Pass," "Yes," "Maybe," or "No," noted on the coverage, depending on each studio's coverage format. Also evaluated is the writer's ability. The screenplay or story may be a "pass" but the writer may be flagged with a "consider," allowing creative executives an introduction to a writer and possible new talent who might be right for another project at the studio. One example of this is a young writer just out of USC named Scott Sturgeon who received "consider" coverage on both his writing ability and his spec screenplay. Two years later, he was hired to rewrite *Black Dog* (1998) when Monika recommended him for the project based upon that positive coverage.

Readers at each studio cover a total of approximately 5,000 submissions each year. Out of those submissions about 250 are recommended and 25-35 optioned by the studio. A handful actually make it to the

"Black Dog" Coverage – First Draft

Type of Material: Screenplay	**Title:** BLACK DOG
Number of Pages: 118 PP	
Number of Scenes:	**Author:** William Mickelberry,
Publisher/Date: ▉▉▉▉	Dan Vining
Submitted by: Anonymous	**Circa:** Present
Submitted to: Anonymous	**Location:** New York and
	Various Southeast
Analyst: ▉▉▉▉	**Genre:** Action Thriller
Date: ▉▉▉▉	**Elements:**

LOGLINE: A former trucker who's suffering the indignities that come with being on parole, gets back into action, but with dire results, when he agrees to drive a load of guns across state lines.

SYNOPSIS: At a truck terminal in Queens, a ferret-like man named LASHLEY, hunts the service bays, looking for JACK CREWS. Lashley finds Crews, a sober man in his 40s, working on a truck engine and immediately begins raking him over the coals, reminding him that with just one word, Lashley can revoke Crews' parole and send him back to prison. But Lashley's cruel baiting is quickly interrupted by CUTLER, Crews' natty, powerfully built boss. Cutler doesn't like the weasely parole-officer harassing one of his men and manhandles him out the door.

Crews is washing up after his shift when Cutler approaches with an ominous offer. He knows Crews is a top notch trucker who lost his license when he went to prison. He offers Crews a chance to get back in the saddle—Cutler will pay him $10,000 to drive a truckload of guns from Georgia, where they are legal, to New York, where they are not. The money is tempting but Crews picks up his 11-year-old daughter, TRACY, from school and takes her home to his ex-wife, MELANIE, and her new husband, SCOOTER, he realizes he can't afford the luxury of thinking only for himself. Crews cares the world for Tracy.

	Excellent	Good	Fair	Poor
Premise		X.............X		
Characterization		X		
Dialogue		X		
Storyline		X.............X		

RECOMMENDATION: <u>CONSIDER</u>
WRITER: <u>CONSIDER</u>

BLACK DOG, by William Mickelberry, Dan Vining

Page 2

Melanie pulls Crews aside and reveals that Scooter has been out of work for months and unless she can come up with $13,000 they'll lose the house and be forced to move to the ghetto. Melanie's plea is genuine and Crews knows what he must do.

Crews returns to Cutler and says he'll take the job, but for $15,000. Cutler agrees but will pay up only on delivery. This done, Crews, takes out a one week life insurance policy for $250,000, made out to Tracy, and flies to Atlanta and makes his way to a remote barn where he finds a gleaming, new semi tractor hitched to a trailer, apparently being guarded by only a calm but imposing pit bull. But, no sooner does Crews climb into the cab than a man in the sleeper compartment sticks a gun against his temple and says "I hope to God you're Jack Crews." The man is EARL, a redneck in a pressed cowboy shirt.

Crews immediately goes to work. He points out that the new, shiny tractor will draw attention and has Earl take him to a local "dealer," a greasy redneck in his 60s named RED, for a trade. Red is more than happy to swap the new tractor for a dirty, battered but otherwise sound one. The unexpected arrival at the barn of a Cadillac bearing a tattooed punk named WES, and his slick sidekick SONNY, throws Crews and he suspects Earl is working a double cross. Earl explains that they'll drive behind the truck as drive back up. It's part of the deal. Crews remains suspicious but gets the rig ready as Wes and Sonny deliver load after load of guns, filling the trailer. A few boxes of toilets go in last, covering the contraband should a cop decide to check out the load. Finally, the pit bull climbs in where he's got food and water stashed behind the boxes, ready to pounce should a cop snoop too far.

The truck and the back up car pull out and hit the interstate. It's immediately clear that Crews is an expert driver...and that he loves driving a big rig truck. It's also clear he just wants to get the job done and over with. It doesn't take long, however for Crews' trepidations about three "partners" to prove well-founded. Wes pulls the Caddy over at the rest stop, supposedly to take a piss. Crews has little choice but to follow suit. Suddenly, a wrecker pulls in and blocks the exit, followed by a sedan bearing Red, his son, GEARY and a couple more rednecks. One of the goons fires a shotgun, blowing off half of Wes' ear, and all hell breaks loose. Crews realizes what's happening and plows the semi rig into the wrecker shoving it out of the way. Although peppered with bullet holes, Crews gets the semi back on the highway and powers off. A heated, bloody chase ensues, ending when Crews forces the pursuing rednecks to plow into a stalled car.

BLACK DOG, by William Mickelberry, Dan Vining

Page 3

After making their escape, Crews trades angry accusations with the "partners," convinced that Wes' need to piss was somehow linked to the attack by the rednecks. What follows is a deadly game in which Red gathers more goons and continues the pursuit, bent on getting the guns and revenge for the death of his son Geary. During a series of bloody shootouts, rammings and crashes, Crews discovers that Earl is Red's son and that Wes has been alerting Red to their whereabouts on a cellular phone. But none of that matters as Red continues the hunt, intent on killing them all. Sonny, mortally wounded, confesses to Crews that he's actually an agent for the ATF, and offers Crews a chance to elude prison if he cooperates and helps the Feds nab Cutler. But Crews is thinking only of getting his money from Cutler and helping Tracy.

He powers the truck through deadly roadblocks, a forest fire and a flash flood and one by one, Red and his goons are killed. Sonny eventually succumbs to his wounds. They reach New York where Earl pulls another fast one, telling Crews the drop off point has changed. Crews manages to dump him out of the truck and phones Cutler, ordering him to meet at the truck terminal as promised...with the money. Crews delivers the goods, and grabs the cash filled briefcase that Cutler hands him. But, as a crew of thugs arrive to take possession of the guns from Cutler, Crews thinks back on what Sonny told him, about how the guns will be used against innocent people in a variety of heinous street crimes. Crews suddenly returns to the semi-tractor, powers it up and drives it into the trailer, causing a fiery explosion that consumes all the guns. Crews then ambles home, only to be accosted by a trio of gangbangers, who shoot him and steal the cash filled briefcase.

Melanie sees a stranger in a suit at her front door and realizes something dire has occurred. He informs her that he needs her signature in order to hand Tracy the benefits of her father's life insurance policy.

BLACK DOG, by William Mickelberry, Dan Vining

Page 4

COMMENT: Gritty, hard-hitting and action packed, this story of a stoic trucker putting everything on the line to help his ex-wife and daughter has the ingredients for a successful, low to medium budget action thriller. It's the kind of blue-collar, macho vehicle that might've starred Burt Reynolds at the beginning of his movie career. The plot is straightforward and not overly complex, stressing the trucker's affinity for his rig and his sense of purpose, as a pretext for the elaborate, violent chase action. There's only so much you can do with high-speed chases between a big rig truck and a variety of pursuit vehicles but these authors manage to come up with some imaginative, spectacular variations.

Crews' quest is rather simple and it's arguably predictable but Crews remains a solid, quietly impressive protagonist whose expertise with a big rig and his Spartan resolve lift his handling of a semi to heroic proportions. His role has dignity and power and he's the kind of close-to-the-vest, man of few words that appeals to action movie fans.

The ambiance of highway action and big rig trucking may seem like the kind of stuff that appeared on screens in the 1970s when trucks and CB radios became a popular but limited genre. While there is some of this quality in this story, its driven more by the interplay between the characters and the escalating air of danger that permeates the chase action. Crews finds himself stuck with a pack of suspicious rednecks, each at the other's throat, each a considerable threat to Crews' desire to get the job done and get the money to his daughter and ex-wife. With the rednecks continually gunning for them, Crews has little choice but to ignore his suspicions as he and his dubious confederates are forced to pull together to survive. The interplay that results has them challenging each other, trading threats, while at the same time they must risk their lives to keep the big rig running. It may seem that the personality conflicts are familiar and stock on one level, but they are deftly written and the dramatic tension that results plays nicely against the action.

This property has aspects that would look good splashed across theatre one-sheets. It also appears to be a relatively low-risk proposition, provided the chase action can be kept within a reasonable budget. The writers make good use of the possibilities for disaster surrounding big rig trucks and play it nicely against the personality of their lead character. It's not art but it is solid, hard-nosed action fare.

CONSIDER

screen. The percentages are astounding! The Writers Guild of America registers over sixty thousand screenplays per year. If the numbers are correct, that means that less than 1 percent of those registered get optioned by a studio in any given year.

With today's computerized technology, it's much easier for the story department to keep tabs on submissions and, with the flick of a button, e-mail executives in minutes when a reader finishes the coverage. Because of this new technology, the database system at a studio is unsurpassed. A story editor can do a query search for potential writers, basketball stories, comedies, crime stories, etc., via the studio's computer database and within seconds come up with a list of writers or movies to present as research for an executive or project. We've come a long way from those early days in Hollywood when file cabinets were loaded to the brim with countless synopses, all carbon-copied for distribution.

WRITING COVERAGE

Coverage is divided into five parts which the reader must be able to formulate concisely and impart the essential information needed to convey the synopsis, premise/logline, the reader's comments, rating box, and recommendation. Basically, all coverage is formatted in a very standard way for most studios and production companies.

Premise/Logline

The premise, or logline, describes the story in one or two sentences, covering the basic concept of the material. The best way to describe a logline is to look in a newspaper's movie listings or in the *TV Guide* and see how a two-hour movie can be reduced to one or two sentences and yet capture the essence of the story. It's also a way of piquing a potential audience member's interest.

Synopsis

The synopsis should convey the tone of the story as well as include all pertinent facts and incidents. Remember, you are telling a story. This should not be more than two pages. Occasionally, especially if a book is covered, a synopsis can be as long as four pages.

Comments

The analysis (comments) page should follow the synopsis. It should be single-spaced and should range from one substantial paragraph to a full

Writing Coverage Instructions

COVERAGE
(top sheet)

Type of Material: SP, N, N (MS) **Title:** TITLE IN CAPS
Number of Pages: length of material
Number of Scenes: if available **Author:** Include all writers on
Publisher/Date: Lone Eagle Pub., 2005   title page
   Based on Novel by John Smith
   tbp: Lone Eagle Pub., 2006

Submitted by: Agent, Producer, Writer **Circa:** When the story takes place

Submitted to: Executive **Location:** Where the story
   takes place

Analyst: Name of Reader **Genre:** Comedy, drama, action
   adventure, sci-fi, etc.

Date: Date writing coverage **Elements:** Director, talent
   attached, COMPARISON
   COVERAGE, WRITING SAMPLE,
   SCENE BREAKDOWN

**LOGLINE or
PREMISE:**   Write a clear one to two sentence description of the story.

COMMENTS: One or two lines of comments

**SYNOPSIS or
SUMMARY:**
- Use courier 12 point typeface
- Present tense
- Describe story as it's happening. Describe opening and closing sequences
- Pick up on any jokes and incorporate them in synopsis
- Pick up all significant plot points

	Excellent	Good	Fair	Poor
Premise				
Characterization				
Dialogue				
Storyline				

RECOMMENDATION: _____
WRITER: _____

(Evaluate the material and writing quality.
Types of recommendations: RECOMMEND, CONSIDER,
NOT RECOMMEND, PASS, YES, NO, MAYBE, CONSIDER CONCEPT)

TITLE IN CAPS / Writer   Date
                                                          Page 2

SYNOPSIS (Continued)

TITLE IN CAPS / Writer   Date
                                                          Page 3

COMMENTS: • Type your strongest opinion and get to the point.
                • Use specific example to illustrate the points.
                • Use boxscores as guideline (premise, characterization,
                  dialogue, storyline, writer evaluation).
                • Avoid run-on sentences.

                • 1st Part: opening argument; general overview of
                  synopsis, small sketch, one sentence (...is an excellent
                  example of.../...is a badly written...). State your reaction.

                • 2nd Part: Characterization. Support argument (The
                  characters are...because everyone can relate...). Focus on
                  biggest problems and strengths. Is the main character
                  interesting? The opponent?

                • 3rd Part: Structure, plot, dialogue.
                  - Storyline: Why storyline is bad (poor structure,
                    no ending, no resolution, why intriguing, why
                    cinematic, why it would make a good or bad film.
                  - Discuss plot problems.
                  - Dialogue: Two sentences. State good or bad. Does it
                    seem real and satisfying?

                • 4th Part: Conclusion or Summary. (This screenplay is a
                  treat to read, however, it won't make a good film
                  because.../...It's commercial because...) Could the script
                  be better with some reworking?

                • Writer evaluation: Weigh how positive and negative
                  your remarks are and on the basis of the whole,
                  choose your recommendation code.

page. The following points should be addressed: premise, characters, relationships, jeopardy, humor, dialogue, and structure. Try to be constructive and think of creative ways to critique. For example, don't say you don't like something without backing it up as to *why* you don't like it. If you make suggestions for how to make the script better, be specific. If the script is not recommended, it's suggested that the reader give the executive one or two positive and three negative comments so the executive can pass on the material politely.

Recommendation Codes

Underneath the comments, type the rating code in capital letters, i.e., RECOMMEND, CONSIDER, NOT RECOMMEND; PASS, YES, MAYBE, NO. Usually there is one line for the screenplay and, under that, there is another line indicating whether the writer should be flagged or recommended. Sometimes the script may be a pass but the writer might be considered.

Rating Box

While it is up to an individual studio or production company to use a box score or grid in their evaluation of a script, these box scores were originally designed to provide a clear and simple evaluation of the written quality of the property. It is divided into ratings of EXCELLENT, GOOD, FAIR, and POOR in which the reader rates the following basic dramatic structural components: premise, characterization, dialogue, and storyline (refers to the plot).

QUESTIONS TO ASK YOURSELF WHILE WRITING COVERAGE AND COMMENTS

Character:
- Does the script have strong characters? Character identification is key to an engaging story.
- Who is the main character (Protagonist)?
- Is he/she believable?
- What is the motivation of the main character?
- Is the journey of the main character realized?
- Do you like the protagonist? Why?
- Who is the Villain (Antagonist)?

- What is the motivation of the villain?
- How does the villain impact the journey of the main character?
- What are the relationships in the script? Are they developed?
- Are the characters interesting? The characters often times are more important to a successful script than structure.

Structure and Story:

- Is the structure fully developed?
- Are all the plot points hit? Are the plot points easy to identify?
- What is the pacing of the script?
- What is your emotional reaction to the ending?
- Does the script have important turning points? For example, *Fatal Attraction* (1987) has an amazing turning point that reels the reader in. The killing of the bunny is the turning point that transforms the Glenn Close character. She changes distinctly from a victim to a vindictive killer.
- Ask yourself if you drop out of the story? When do you lose interest? Most often this can be due to poor character development.
- Are there any distracting holes in the logic?

General Questions:

- What is the setting? The time period?
- Does the setting and time period add to the script? How are they important to the story?
- What is the genre of the script? Does the script remain true to the genre? (If it is a comedy, are you delighted? A horror film, are you scared? A thriller, on the edge of your seat?)
- Does the script make you cry, laugh, or be afraid?
- How is the dialogue? Is it trite, honest, boring, etc.?
- How do you feel at the end of the story? The script should have you feeling a certain way by the end. What do you feel? Do you feel anything? Was it the intended emotion? Overall, are you invested in the story? The script should make you feel something or get you emotionally involved. Does it accomplish that?

OTHER TYPES OF COVERAGE AND SUBMISSIONS

Comparison Coverage

For comparison coverage, a reader lists the significant differences between a previous synopsis, and the latest draft of the screenplay. Using the coverage top sheet format (as illustrated above), the reader writes a detailed and paginated notation in lieu of writing a new synopsis. While minor description or dialogue changes are not significant; all other changes should be considered worthy of mention. After listing the changes, a full comment page or analysis of the impact of the script revisions should follow, with the reader stating whether the changes worked and what else needs to be done to further the next draft. On the top sheet, in the elements section, the reader would indicate that the work is a comparison coverage.

Writing Sample

When evaluating a screenplay as a writing sample, a reader indicates under "elements" that the work is a writing sample, and then writes a top sheet and synopsis. When writing the comments, however, the reader should carefully analyze the screenplay's basic elements (character, dialogue, structure, plot) and include an evaluation of the writer(s) ability to successfully render each of these areas. The comments should conclude with a recommendation that further submissions by the writer(s) be considered or not recommended, with special attention to specific strengths and weaknesses.

Unsolicited Material

Material that does not come in through the normal professional channels (i.e., an agent, a producer, or an entertainment lawyer) is considered "unsolicited material" and, for legal reasons, cannot be read by the story department without the required release form being signed. Rejection letters are usually prepared by the legal department and sent with the material back to the source, unread.

A DAY IN THE LIFE OF THE STORY DEPARTMENT

With a usual story department turnaround time of three days, a script is submitted, read, coverage is delivered to the story editor, and the coverage and script are then returned with the project to the executive who requested it. This is all done under the auspices of the story department.

Comparison Coverage Sample

Type of Material: Screenplay
Number of Pages: 110
Number of Scenes:
Publisher/Date:

Submitted by: Producer

Submitted to: Executive

Analyst: Name of Reader

Date: Date writing coverage

Title: BLACK DOG

Author: William Mickelberry,
Dan Vining

Circa: Present

Location: New York and
Various Southeast

Genre: Action Thriller

Elements: COMPARISON COVERAGE

LOGLINE: A former trucker, who's suffering the indignities that come with being on parole, gets back into action, but with dire results, when he agrees to drive a load of guns across state lines.

Please see (date of previous coverage) for synopsis. The new draft incorporates the following changes:

1. The new draft contains a new opening scene with the ATF agents and a high-speed chase.

2. CREWS is now in his 30s instead of 40s.

3. MELANIE, Crews' ex-wife, is not re-married to SCOOTER.

4. TRACY is now 13 instead of 11.

5. RED's son is named JUNIOR instead of GEARY and is introduced earlier in the story.

6. The life insurance policy is for fifteen days instead of a week and no amount is mentioned.

7. The last scene of TRACY playing basketball replaces the one with Melanie receiving word about the life insurance policy.

	Excellent	Good	Fair	Poor
Premise		X.............X		
Characterization		X		
Dialogue		X		
Storyline		X.............X		

RECOMMENDATION: __CONSIDER__
WRITER: __CONSIDER__

However, what happens when a script is submitted to a studio? What is the process? You'd be surprised at how many hands fondle a script and/or its coverage, or how many eyes have, at the very least, seen the title and writer's name on reports before the material is returned to the sender.

Upon receipt of material for consideration, a development executive's assistant fills out an internal interoffice submission form that accompanies the material throughout its stay at the studio. The project is then sent to the story department and the ball is set in motion.

The assistant story editor or the coverage assistant double-checks the database for any previous coverage written on the screenplay by that writer or title. If there is previous coverage on a different draft, the material would be re-read and re-covered as comparison coverage and considered a resubmission. That means that a new top sheet would be added, listing the significant changes either in numeric order or with bullets, and placed on top of the earlier coverage. A new comment page would also be written and attached in which the reader would note if this draft worked better than the first draft. If two names are found referring to the same writer, the assistant will handle the material as a resubmission. The new name would be added in parentheses under the writer's name on the original synopsis. Titles and writers are always cross-referenced. And you thought you could get away with a pseudonym!

Material is logged into a computer database by title, writer, submitter, development executive, date received in story department, a due date, and can be sorted on a Daily Coverage Submission Report.

The assistant story editor then prioritizes the material by one of the following due dates:

- *Immediate/RUSH read*—It's handled immediately, read quickly, and given a verbal response to the executive with coverage following;
- *Day read*—It's read and written up by the end of that day;
- *Overnight read*—It's read overnight so that coverage is e-mailed and/or on the executive's desk by 8:00 a.m.;
- *Weekend read*—It's read over the weekend and coverage is e-mailed and/or on the executive's desk by 8:00 a.m. Monday morning.

Material submitted to the head of production is given top priority. A screenplay submitted by a well-known producer or agent will be given precedence.

Enter the reader who is then assigned his or her material. These days, most screenplays are submitted as a pdf. Should the executive receive a hard copy, that copy is converted into a pdf file and submitted electronically so it is available to both the reader and the executive. The reader spends a couple of hours reading the material on the computer and a couple of hours writing the synopsis and comment, returning the coverage electronically to the story department.

Upon returning the coverage, the story editor or assistant story editor checks it for spelling errors. Distribution of the coverage is electronically sent back to the executive who requested the coverage. With new technology, story departments are computerized and coverage is filed in the main database system for storage and immediate retrieval. Until the mid to late 1990s, coverage was filed in metal filing cabinets by title or given a numeric code (which included the year plus the submission number, i.e., 971032 meaning 1997 and it was the 1,032nd submission that year).

Once the coverage is turned in, the paperwork and e-mails whiz around the story department in all kinds of reports. For example, if the material is rated CONSIDER or RECOMMEND, the assistant makes extra copies to be filed for the consider coverage report. In fact, some story departments create files and circulate several different kinds of reports throughout the creative group including:

- *Weekend Read Report*—A memo listing projects on the weekend read broken down by studio projects and spec screenplays, novels, and coverage.
- *Daily Submission Report*—Submissions sent to the story department for coverage are sometimes recorded on both a daily and weekly report to provide creative group executives with information of what is submitted to the studio for consideration.
- *Project Development Report*—This report lists all the projects optioned and purchased that the studio is developing. It lists all the talent involved including writers, producers, directors, source material, optional/committed draft steps, creative and business affairs executives attached to the project, logline, etc.
- *Project Status Report*—Projects are listed by phases: (a) pending release dates, (b) post-production, (c) production, (d) pre-production, (e) projects close to a greenlight or priority development, (f) active development, (g) recent projects abandoned, in turnaround, or inactive projects. Reports vary depending on the company or studio.
- *Consider Coverage Report*—Coverage that receives a "consider" or "recommend" is listed on a memo with genre, title, writer, and the executive's initials.

Weekend Read Report Sample

WEEKEND READ MEMO

DATE: Friday date

TO: Creative Group

FROM: Story Department or Story Editor's name

SUBJECT: WEEKEND READS

COPIES: Creative Group Executives

STUDIO/COMPANY PROJECTS	NEXT STEP
I DON'T GET IT by Gilroy Shafer (XX)	Optional polish
SLOW BURN by Coleen Woodman (XX)	Committed 1st rew
GUILTY PLEASURE by Sandy Olsen (XX)	SYNOPSIS ONLY

SCREENPLAYS	
MESSAGE FOR UNCLE by Ben Tennant (XX)	MM/GT/KD
*GLUE by Cindy Greely (XX)	RE/MS/NS/AP
ZIP THE BIRD by S.B. Sawyer (XX)	CC/ZD/MM
*FORCED OUT by Bill Miller (XX/XX)	KD/GT/NS/RE
DATING BLUES by Cloe Carpenter (XX)	MS/ZD

SYNOPSES/TREATMENTS

THE TIME TRAVELER'S WIFE Novel by Audrey Niffenegger (XX)

SUPERKID comic book by Del Reed (XX)

JERSEY RED article by Leon Rogers (XX)

UNTITLED BOB SMART SCREENPLAY by Bob Smart (XX)

ROOM FOR GLEN by Gordon North (XX)

*coverage to follow Monday

Consider Coverage Report Sample

CONSIDER COVERAGE AND/OR WRITERS

DATE: Current Date

TO: Creative Group Executives

FROM: Story Department or Story Editor's name

SUBJECT: CONSIDER COVERAGE & WRITERS

COPIES: Creative Group Executives & Story Analysts

COMEDY
RED COOL CAR by Peter Smith (based on N by Tony Clark) (XX)

ROMANTIC COMEDY
WIN A TRIP TO PATAGONIA by Victor Lewis (XX)

DRAMA/COMEDY
AGAINST THE MUSIC by Robin Edwards (XX)

SCI-FI/DRAMA
THE FINAL EXAM by Beth Meredith (XX)

DRAMA/THRILLER
COOPER by Darrin Moore (XX)
TRAPPED IN SILENCE by Eric Rand (XX)
SEEK THE THRILL by Andy Jones (XX)

ACTION/ADVENTURE
INTO THE WILD by Victoria Dicks (XX)

w/s = consider writing sample

Once the coverage is turned in, the process begins all over again with readers being assigned new submissions to cover and executives evaluating potential movies via coverage and screenplays.

CONCLUSION

The story department is a complex system that keeps the studio's creative team in-the-know. It provides an invaluable resource of stories and writers in addition to recording the day-to-day operations of the creative process. The relationships, knowledge, education, and access you are allowed in a studio story department is the perfect introduction for anyone who wants to produce, become a development executive, or run a studio in Hollywood some day. It creates an opportunity for its staff to move up the ladder into the executive suites of the studio.

As long as there is material to be submitted, the story department will continue to buzz, supplying executives with the much-needed synopses and comments on everything submitted to the studio.

EXERCISE 1

Rent the movie *BLACK DOG* (1998)—Read the coverage of *BLACK DOG* in this chapter. Note the differences. Write a comparison coverage.

EXERCISE 2

Pick three movies and write a logline for each of them.

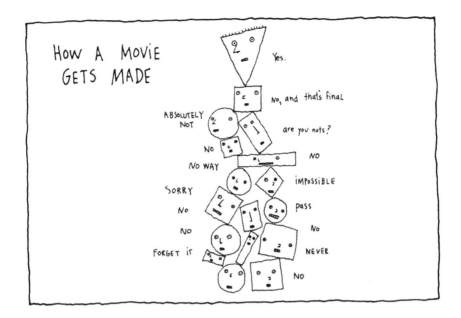

4

"So Many Titles, So Many Decision Makers"
the studio creative executives

In the previous chapter, you've been introduced to all the players who work in the story department at a studio. Amazingly, there are even more creative executives in positions higher than the story department—all of whom have a significant and specific role in making movies. There are executive vice presidents, senior vice presidents, vice presidents, directors of development, creative executives ("CEs" for short)—it may seem like the studios are top heavy with employees, but think about it: there has to be a considerable staff handling all the projects, especially if you want your executives to get some rest at night. If, as we stated previously, there are approximately 5,000 submissions to individual studios a year, and approximately 25 to 35 of those submissions are put into development—in addition to the projects that are *already* in development—you need a creative executive team overseeing a slate of 150 to 300 projects, all of which are in different phases of development. Further, you need a large team overseeing these projects because one executive may be supervising twenty to forty projects at any given time. Most studios have at least two executives on each project: a junior and a senior executive. These projects are all at different stages of development and/or production, requiring the development executives' attention to initiate and oversee first drafts, rewrites, and polishes. Additionally, the development executive must continue to seek and attach talent for open writing and directing assignments, and oversee all phases of production, including: pre-production, casting, production, viewing dailies, post-production, and delivery to the studio of the finished product.

During the development phase, the goal is to flag those projects that are further along for potential production but may be on hold for one reason or another. One example would be if a studio has a project that has a director attached to it and they're waiting on a particular star's schedule—that project would be called "attempting to greenlight" or "priority development" because the movie will get a greenlight as soon as the element, in this case the star, is available. Another instance is if the studio is aiming for a particular release slot (i.e., a summer blockbuster or fall Oscar contender).

A production or development vice president may also be involved in testing their movie to sneak preview audiences. These audiences are usually made up of the general public at a commercial movie theatre. The information gained from sneak previews provides the necessary input required for designing the film's marketing and distribution plans. These previews may also point out problems with the story and sometimes the filmmakers (along with the studio) may try and rectify them before general release.

Executives also service "producer term deals" on the lot. This means a producer and/or production company has a deal with the studio in which they are either:

1) *Exclusive* to the studio, meaning they can only sell a project to one studio. This may sound exciting but it has its limitations in that once a studio passes on a project, that producer cannot take it to another studio. Deals like this are rare in today's market.

2) *A first look deal*, meaning they must give their studio the first opportunity to see and fund the project. The studio must pass on it within a certain time parameter before the producer is allowed to try and sell it to a competing studio. The vast majority of deals today are first look deals.

3) *A second look deal* happens sometimes when a powerful producer is able to secure not only a first look deal at one studio but a second look deal at another studio. They still have to show the project to the first look deal first but they have a backup studio also paying for the opportunity to buy another studio's rejects.

In return for this "allegiance," the producer's overhead (office, support staff, a development exec, office equipment, supplies, and messengers) are paid for, in part or full, by the studio, depending on the caliber of the producer. This, however, is just an advance against any film that the producer or production company makes. Once the movie is made, the expenses for this overhead are recouped from the film's budget and/or film revenues.

Sometimes producers are even given a "discretionary fund," which gives the company a sum of money each year, the amount of which is negotiated in that production company's deal with the studio. With this money, they can buy projects on their own and develop them in-house, without studio input, until they deem the project ready to be seen by the studio. From this point, the hope is that the project will be put into development, and, eventually, financed for full production by the studio. However, discretionary funds are becoming more and more scarce in this economy. So, aside from canvassing the town for new material, finding new talent, and overseeing what's already on the development roster, a development or production executive at a studio has to also take care of, or service the producers who already have deals at the studio.

But who are all those people, with all those titles, who have such an influence on the decision to option or purchase material? What exactly do they do?

Keeping in mind that every studio may differ, here's a quick rundown by title of the powers that be in the motion picture division of a studio:

- *Chairman of the Motion Picture Group*—Has the greenlight power to say "yes" to production of a movie.
- *President of Production or Co-Presidents of Production*—Approves material put into development.
- *Vice Presidents* (This includes *Executive Vice President of Production, Senior Vice President of Production, Vice President of Creative Affairs* or *Development*)—Oversees movies in production and development, oversees producer term deals, listens to pitches from writers and finds new material.

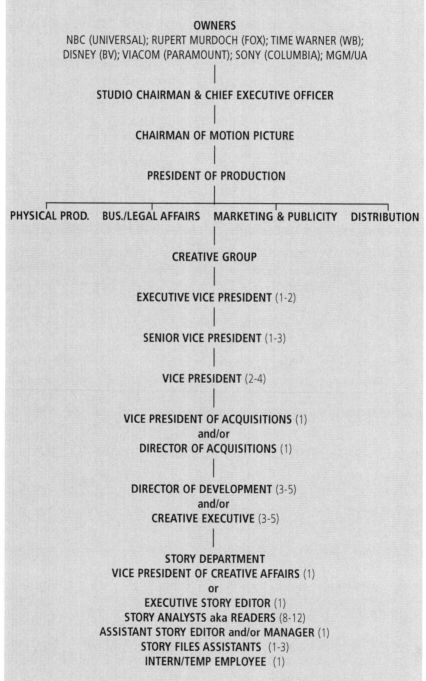

EXECUTIVES AND POSITIONS AT THE STUDIO MOTION PICTURE GROUP

OWNERS
NBC (UNIVERSAL); RUPERT MURDOCH (FOX); TIME WARNER (WB);
DISNEY (BV); VIACOM (PARAMOUNT); SONY (COLUMBIA); MGM/UA

STUDIO CHAIRMAN & CHIEF EXECUTIVE OFFICER

CHAIRMAN OF MOTION PICTURE

PRESIDENT OF PRODUCTION

PHYSICAL PROD.   BUS./LEGAL AFFAIRS   MARKETING & PUBLICITY   DISTRIBUTION

CREATIVE GROUP

EXECUTIVE VICE PRESIDENT (1-2)

SENIOR VICE PRESIDENT (1-3)

VICE PRESIDENT (2-4)

VICE PRESIDENT OF ACQUISITIONS (1)
and/or
DIRECTOR OF ACQUISITIONS (1)

DIRECTOR OF DEVELOPMENT (3-5)
and/or
CREATIVE EXECUTIVE (3-5)

STORY DEPARTMENT
VICE PRESIDENT OF CREATIVE AFFAIRS (1)
or
EXECUTIVE STORY EDITOR (1)
STORY ANALYSTS aka READERS (8-12)
ASSISTANT STORY EDITOR and/or MANAGER (1)
STORY FILES ASSISTANTS (1-3)
INTERN/TEMP EMPLOYEE (1)

(1-2) Parenthesis = people in position

- *Vice President or Director of Acquisitions*—Some studios have acquisition executives or an off-shoot or subsidiary company (i.e., Universal's Focus Features, Fox's Searchlight, etc.) who scour film festivals and film markets looking for movies already made to distribute. Sometimes these films are submitted as screenplays with "elements," i.e., attached director, stars, and/or producers along with a budget and sometimes with a promo reel.

- *Director of Production, Director of Development, Director of Creative Affairs, Creative Executive*—Assists a vice president with films in production and development. Usually writes a set of development notes on various projects, correlates the executive's input into one set of notes as well as any other tasks requested by a vice president. They usually have an emphasis on finding newer talent and staying on top of new material including screenplays, books, and true-life stories, commonly called "tracking," sent out by production companies and agencies.

Tracking is a way for executives to pursue new or upcoming material and then keep tabs on their status so they can be the first one to have the material submitted to their company or studio. This requires a lot of networking with both book and film agents, having good relationships with writers, and being aware of what's going to be "hot." Not that many years ago, it was all done by phone or weekly gatherings at restaurants in which executives from production companies and studios would mingle with each other and share information.

Today, tracking is done mostly via the Internet through what is called tracking boards. Though most tracking board members are from production companies, studio executives have been known to belong to them as well and keep tabs on the material that is going out to the town. You may ask yourself why competing companies would share this information. They do because it's better to be included at the party than to be the wall-flower. Think of it this way: by helping each other, they help themselves. Information is a powerful tool and the more information you have, the more options and inroads you can make.

Studios look for development and production executives who are energetic, have a love of movies, have a great eye for hip new talent, are able to foresee trends, have solid production experience, networking, and people skills along with writing ability, and a talent for developing stories into film. Successful executives know how to express themselves in a constructive way and can succinctly convey their opinions in ways that don't

From THE MOVING PICTURE WORLD Magazine circa 1911-1914, a precursor to production charts

LICENSED
FILM STORIES

SELIG

THE RUBBER INDUSTRY ON THE AMAZON (July 25)—
The first scenes show how the rubber tree is tapped in the early morning, and how the sap is gathered at noon. Then comes scenes showing how the sap is congealed in the smoke from nuts of palm trees, until it becomes what the natives term a "biscuit." Next we are shown views of the world's largest rubber market, Manaos, Brazil, twenty-three hundred miles from the mouth of the Amazon. Here the biscuit is searched thoroughly for impurities. The last scenes show the receiving and packing of the "biscuits" at the wharf.

THE TALE OF A SOLDIER'S RING (July 27)—
In the first scene of this play, laid in the grounds of a noted and splendid Colonial mansion in Georgia, Marion Dunlap is betrothed to Robert Alroy, who places a diamond ring upon his sweetheart's finger. The Civil War has begun, and Marion returns the ring to Alroy and ends their engagement, when Alroy enlists in a Union regiment. Marion and her mother visit Miss Carrington at Philamont in Virginia. The fortunes of war brings Alroy's regiment near Philamont. In a skirmish with Confederate troops, Alroy's reconnoitering party is annihilated, and Alroy takes refuge in the Carrington mansion. Confederate officers make their headquarters in the same house.

Hidden in the fireplace, Alroy hears the Confederate officers discuss their plans, and when they go out to dinner, he secures their campaign map and escapes to the woods. Chased and severely wounded by Confederate patrols, Alroy re-enters the Carrington mansion.

Marion finds her former lover in a swoon, and assisted by Abraham, the Negro butler, she secretes him under the bed in her room. When the pursuing Confederates enter and question her, Marion answers that the "Yank is not there." Later, in dressing Alroy's wound, the girl finds the missing map. She denounces Alroy as a spy and holds him up with his own revolver. Alroy faints and Marion, touched by his condition, helps him to escape after she has returned the stolen map. Peace, which makes ours a reunited country, restores Marion to her lover, and in a beautiful, romantic scene, Alroy again places the ring upon the finger of his sweetheart.

EDISON

THE DOOMED SHIP (July 28)—
Dick, a sailor lad, woos and wines Mabel: the daughter of a hard, miserly shipping merchant. Dick, in order to get some money before getting married, secures a position as mate on a coasting vessel. The ship happens to belong to his prospective father-in-law who has received a report that she is in very bad condition and must not leave port. He pays little attention to this report, and lets her sail. But before doing so, he writes a note to his future son-in-law, to come and see him. Dick also receives a letter from Mabel, to meet her before he sails. He pays no attention to the old man's letter, and after leaving his sweetheart, sails away.

The report reaches the old miser that ship and crew have been dazed to pieces. It kills the old miser, and almost kills his daughter. As luck would have it, Dick is the sole survivor. He finds his sweetheart at their trysting place, brooding over her loss. This is suddenly dispelled by her lover's strong arms about her. It is needless to say that they are eventually married.

BIOGRAPH

THE PEDDLER'S BAG (Sept 17)—
The wayward son of a landed gentleman persecutes the gamekeeper's wife with his attentions, and, in the husband's absence, bribes the village peddler to carry him into the cottage in a bag. Cutting his way out at dead of night, he alarms the wife, who seizes a gun and shoots, then flees in panic. The gamekeeper, suspicious, hastens home in time to be suspected by those who find the body, is arrested and brought to trial on the evidence of the butler, who has heard him threaten the young master. At a dramatic moment, the signed statement of his wife and the arrest of the peddler bring about his release.

MURPHY AND THE MERMAIDS (Sept 19)—
Murphy's wife sets him to chopping wood while she goes swimming with their daughter. A Hebrew peddler, who happens along, is forced by Murphy to chop wood. Murphy nailing a revolver to the barn so that it looks as if has the peddler covered. Murphy goes fishing, falls asleep and dreams of mermaids. His wife and daughter find him and chase him home, where all three are met by the peddler, who has discovered the trick and armed himself with the revolver.

GAUMONT

A SOCIETY MOTHER (July 25)—
Tabor, anxious that her daughter should make a good match, takes her to the Ambassador's ball; where she is introduced to a wealthy suitor, by whom she is much admired.

offend writers and producers. They understand the etiquette of giving notes to writers and know how to motivate writers to do the changes necessary in order to get the greenlight.

During the development stages, they read writing samples to assist in filling open writing assignments (novels, or magazine articles that need to be adapted into screenplays, scripts in development at the studio that need new writers hired for rewrites), watch director reels to fill open directing assignments (movies moving closer to production or that already have a greenlight and are in need of a director), and prepare potential talent lists. Talent lists usually include a target list of actors, writers, and/or directors, their agent/manager information, status availability (if they're shooting a film and/or when their next film is scheduled to start), along with their most recent credit. These lists are used to attach talent, check availability of talent, and/or to replace talent (for example, replacing a writer for the next draft of the screenplay if it's needed). There are many Internet Web sites with search capabilities that can supply this information, which will be further covered in the Resources chapter.

A talent list would include the information below:
- Title of project
- Type of list (Actor list, Actress list, Director's list, Writer's list)
- Name of talent (Actor, Actress, Director or Writer)
- Agent and/or Manager
- Current status section listing the phase of availability. (Either they are *Available*; in *Post-production*; *Shooting*; or in *Pre-production*) Include the title of the movie, the studio (abbreviated i.e., FOX, UNIV, PAR, WB, COL, DIS), and the start date with the month and year if they are in Pre-production.

One Example of a Talent List

TITLE OF PROJECT		
TYPE OF LIST (ACTOR, ACTRESS, DIRECTOR, and/or WRITER)		
"Character Name" (if an actor or actress list)		
NAME	AGENT AND/OR MANAGER	STATUS
Joe Hollywood	John Deal/All Talent Agency	(Either they are Available; in Post-Production; Shooting or in Pre-Production

A DAY IN THE LIFE OF A STUDIO DEVELOPMENT EXECUTIVE

From the moment they rise in the morning, sometimes with a script in their hand, vice presidents and creative executives usually start their days with breakfast meetings followed by lunches, drinks, and dinner meetings with agents, managers, producers, directors, and/or writers. Between these meetings, they may have screenplays to evaluate, which require a day read. They capitalize on their film relationships and contacts to scout material to bring into their companies. Needless to say, they are on the phone constantly "rolling calls"—a slang term for returning or making phone calls.

If that isn't enough, mornings are spent in weekly creative group meetings—such as weekend read meetings, business affairs meetings, or development meetings to go over the submissions, the deals already or about to be in place, and the movies that are about to go or are already in production. They take pitch meetings on new projects, keep up with up-and-coming talent by either reading writing samples or watching directors' reels, take development meetings to brainstorm with writers and producers on projects already in development...and still may try to find the time to attend a screening or a sneak preview in the evening. Sometimes they have an overnight read or if it's a Friday, a stack of weekend reading to get through.

When projects are in production, their responsibilities also involve viewing dailies of their films. Dailies are the printed takes of a movie already in production, shot the day before. Usually they arrive the day after they've been shot from wherever that movie is shooting, for viewing by studio executives or producers who may not be on location. Dailies are also viewed by producers and executives who are on set; they are used to judge the actor's performances, lighting, scenic design, determine how a scene is set up, or to control production costs. It's also a way for the studio to make sure the movie is turning out the way they want it to turn out. If the performances or direction is not coming through, the dailies serve as a way for the studio to determine whether to re-shoot a scene, replace a director or actor, and/or bring in someone else before the budget runs away with itself. It also gives the studio the opportunity to talk to the director and producer if they don't like the direction the film is taking (e.g. the tone of the piece, the lead actor's performance, the look of the film, etc.) and to try and fix the problems in future scenes before the shooting ends. Today's new digital technology has made screening dailies faster, easier, and less expensive.

The networking and overseeing of material from script to screen make up the studio executive's life.

DEVELOPMENT NOTES

Aside from buying new material, one of the most important job functions a studio executive has is giving development notes. There is no wrong or right way to write development notes and each studio and production company has their own structure. In addition, every executive or producer has their own opinion on how to make a story better. However, most movie plotlines derive from ancient storytelling structure. The granddaddy of all the writing books is still Aristotle's *Poetics*, written more than 2,000 years ago, and still followed to this day. This thin little book that has been the literary handbook for centuries is still the best in its genre for describing the natural way of storytelling. There is a beginning, a middle, and an end. Then, there's the journey the characters must go through in order to get to each point on the structure map, taking left and right turns through the plotline so as to make the story less predictable and more compelling.

With so many books written on the structure of storytelling, Aristotle's closest contemporary rival is Lajos Egri, a Hungarian who wrote *The Art of Dramatic Writing*, originally titled *How to Write a Play*, and published in 1942. Around 1921, Georges Polti, a famous French literary critic and academic, rendered there are thirty-six dramatic situations that correspond to thirty-six emotional conflicts, their action and interaction. Though not written down, it was in fact eighteenth century Italian author, Carlo Gozzi (*Turandot)* who is credited with finding the thirty-six dramatic situations. Polti rediscovered them and published a book about them called *The Thirty-Six Dramatic Situations*. Others believe there are only seven basic plotlines, and it's how you execute them that makes them unique:

- Person against Nature (*The Day After Tomorrow*, 2004)
- Person against Person (*The Last Samurai*, 2003)
- Person against Environment (*Falling Down*, 1993)
- Person against Machines/Technology (*I, Robot*, 2004)
- Person against the Supernatural (*The Blair Witch Project*, 1999)
- Person against Self (*Adaptation*, 2002)
- Person against God/Religion (*Saved*, 2004)

While this is not a book on screenwriting, it helps to know some of the basic ideas of structure, which will be touched upon throughout this book in chapters such as *Finding New Ideas* and *The Art of Pitching*.

Development notes should be geared toward helping the writer find the direction to rewrite and fix problematic areas of the material, thus making it stronger. It is never easy giving notes to writers. The executive has to have the ability to convince them that what he or she is saying is for the good of the movie and the writer's story. Creative executives must be able to point out the flaws or holes in a screenplay and suggest ways to fix them without having the writer get defensive or hurt.

Filmmaking is a collaborative medium. From the beginning of the studio system, the movie moguls always gave their two cents worth of constructive criticism. Development notes came full circle in the early 1980s rein of Jeffrey Katzenberg, Michael Eisner, and the late Don Simpson when they ruled Paramount Pictures. They structured notes in a memorandum format and started asking readers to do notes on projects. They then hired creative executives, who later became successful producers in their own right, including Michael Besman, Richard Fischoff, David Kirkpatrick, Laurence Mark, Lora Lee, and the late Dawn Steel. Some of these executives wrote pages and pages (sometimes ten to twenty pages of notes) depending on the project and its needs. For example, in 1982, one set of development notes for the movie *Footloose* (1984) was twenty-two pages long. It included a two-page overview that articulated the studio's point of view and offered suggestions for further improving the present draft. They stressed that nothing is etched in stone and the memo should be viewed as a starting point for further discussion. Some of the notes included clearly defining the focus of the movie and the concern that attention had been diffused among too many characters, relationships, issues, and events. As a result, they wanted the audience to come away with a stronger understanding of what the movie was about thematically. This was followed by very specific page notes—all with the intention of backing up the studio's overview. Two years later, *Footloose* was released. Today, studio notes are usually four to ten pages but the formatting remains virtually the same as it did over twenty years ago.

There is great debate as to whether these development notes have helped or hindered the art of making movies. Some believe this format of notes has only served to stray from the filmmaker's vision, creating "movies made by committee" rather than relying on the producer, the writer, and, eventually, the director to realize the vision. Could this be the root of formulaic and homogenized studio fare? Even so, it is important to acknowledge that studio development notes are here to stay, and executives, writers, directors, and producers must work within the studio system utilizing this format—for better or for worse.

Keeping the many differing viewpoints in mind, we will now move on to discuss at length development notes and how to write them. Notes are a required aspect of today's industry and hopefully, we will give you the ammunition you need to address the best way to give these notes while keeping in mind the original vision and integrity of the written word.

Development notes are always addressed from the studio to the producers and/or writer. While some studios differ slightly in format today, they usually begin with a general overview on how pleased the studio is to be involved with the project and then move on to more specific notes and suggestions. These notes serve as a basis for discussion and brainstorming when the studio executive and producer or writer next meet. The notes would mostly focus on the structure, Act I, Act II, Act III, turning points, the characters, and relationships. Lastly, there may be a section of specific page notes listing the script page number along with suggestions and ideas for strengthening the story, characters, and dialogue.

An Example of Page Notes

Page 28   We need to see more sympathy for our lead character in this scene.

Page 42   While this cutaway to the FBI/ATM operation is good, this subplot needs to start earlier.

Page 89   We like this discussion of the Black Dog phenomenon very much, but feel we should be getting this information much earlier in the story.

Notes identify the problem areas. They might raise inconsistencies in the story or suggest more character development is needed. If some of the plotting is confusing, notes may question those plot points in order to help the writer pinpoint the work that needs to be done. They may propose a stronger or a different story structure or recommend that a character have a stronger point of view. They define the problem, examine why there is a problem, and discover ways to fix the problem. With each new draft, the executive must evaluate whether the characters are good characters, what is the "spark," and what's the best way to express the main idea of the script? Is the story realistic, plausible, and accessible? Do the characters move the plot forward and come alive? Is the middle related to the end and does it progress smoothly? Is the script commercial or marketable? If something doesn't make sense, the executive must think about what is in the writer's head that isn't making it onto the page.

When discussing a script with a writer or producer, it is best to begin by pointing out the things that are working. People will respond more positively to encouragement than they do to straight criticism. All too often, notes are given only as criticism, and the writer walks away feeling like nothing is working. Praise goes a long way toward helping the writer to listen better and be willing to address the other areas that need work.

Writers have many temperaments and it is important to distinguish their personalities. For example, if a writer is very quiet, it would behoove the producer or executive to engage the writer in a brainstorming session, getting them to talk by asking questions. If a writer is long-winded, the producer or executive might try to help the writer "cut to the chase" a little bit faster. Being on the same page, so to speak, will prevent the development of two very different screenplays. We can't tell you how many times a screenplay has been delivered and the script is nowhere near the concept originally bought or discussed by the studio or network—all because the writer was on a different wavelength than we had thought.

It is also important to engage the writer and/or producer to brainstorm with the executive on some of the suggestions he or she is making, because sometimes a better idea comes along that is prodded by the original suggestion. Don't just criticize their work, but rather discuss ways it can be made better.

THINKING LIKE A DEVELOPMENT EXECUTIVE

As already discussed, most development notes begin with a general overview or introductory paragraph, followed by bulleting the problematic areas. It is with these bullets that the development executive backs up these highlighted problems with an explanation of how to improve or resolve the issues.

While reading a script, think about the areas that cause you to react negatively, what works for you, what doesn't, the areas where you get bored or start to lose interest, and, finally, the things about the story you just don't buy "as real" or feel contrived. Jot down your reactions and then structure the big problems with big bullet points.

Development executives should find the one problem from which all others stem. Find the voice or idea that sparks the script and focus on that. Notes should not just list the problems, but should focus on the things that may actually fix the problems in the story. Always try phrasing your notes in a positive way. For example, instead of saying, "this scene is weak and needs work," it would be better to offer a solution or suggestion that is positive, like, "we might get more out of this scene if the lead did this..." Rather than saying, "I don't like the protagonist, he's too dull and boring, and I have no sympathy for him," try to give suggestions with a positive spin like, "the protagonist is too one-dimensional, give him a scene where he shows some positive traits. Make us like him and feel for him." Suggest changes to create a stronger screenplay. Notes should be looked at as a way to improve the screenplay, not to hinder or change it from its original intention.

Come up with your own ideas and solutions to make the script work better. Never make it an argument of why the script should not be made into a movie but instead explain how addressing these notes *will* make it a "movie." The fact is that the story was placed into development because some executive or creative group saw its potential as a movie. The reader's coverage deals with why a story *shouldn't* be made into a movie. If you are doing development notes already, you are way past that point. Now, it is about improving it and readying it in order to push it towards a greenlight picture. So roll up your sleeves, this is the real work.

TYPES OF DEVELOPMENT NOTES

While each studio may do things a little differently, the basic overall system remains the same. Keeping that in mind, here are a few types of development notes utilized in the studio system:

(1) *Story Department Project Notes*—Some studios have readers do project notes. Usually the notes are a discussion of the script, identifying what works and what doesn't work, and offering concrete solutions. This is where you can often recognize how the screenplay has possibly strayed from the original vision for the movie.

(2) *Vision Notes*—How do the executive and studio see the movie? What are the big changes? What does the creative executive team think the story needs to be in order to sell it, get it made, and have it succeed at the box office?

(3) *Draft Notes*—Identifying, in detail, the notes that are to be tackled in a new draft or specific rewrite.

(4) *Page Notes*—Specific notes by page number.

Development Notes Format—How to Structure Them

MEMORANDUM

DATE: Date of Memo

TO: Producers and/or Writer

FROM: The Studio

SUBJECT: TITLE OF PROJECT by Writer, Current draft of
Screenplay, Date of Screenplay

(Overview or Introduction paragraph)
We are pleased to be involved with **TITLE OF PROJECT**. It is our feeling that we are well on our way toward creating a terrific action comedy that has wide audience appeal. In an effort to make the best possible movie, we have outlined a number of suggestions, which might even further improve the present screenplay. First off, while the screenplay is developing well, there may be ways to heighten the comedy without losing the throughline of the story. Even though these characters do extraordinary things, they should be rooted in reality in order for the comedy to work. The problem of John's leaving and then returning has not been solved. However, John's character remains problematic in that he is more reactive than active. The structure of the storyline kicks off strongly in the first act but loses steam by the third act. While Bob and Mary have great rapport and witty dialogue, we need to have a better understanding of why they are attracted to each other.

Please keep in mind that these are merely suggestions and should serve as a basis for discussion when we next meet. In general, we need to focus on the following areas:

(Organize your greater points with bullets)
- Structure—developing a stronger storyline and heightening the comedy.
- Strengthening Bob and Mary's characters' attraction and working as a team.
- Deepening John's character.
- The third act needs to be more climactic and satisfying.

(Back up your points)

Developing a stronger storyline
The premise of TITLE OF PROJECT is a terrific one. In order to more fully realize this premise, we feel that certain story beats need to be heightened (***back this up in your page notes***). Such intensification, we believe, will help us create a stronger, cleaner storyline.

Strengthening Bob and Mary's characters and working as a team
It is not clear why Bob is attracted to Mary. We need to set up their relationship stronger and see them work as a team. Perhaps a...

Deepening John's character
John is too passive and is too much of a one-note character. He needs to have...

The third act needs to be more climactic and satisfying
The sequence at the end needs to complete the action and tension that precedes it. While we like the confrontation scene very much, and think the script is improved by moving it to the house, the denouement still feels anticlimactic.

Specific Page Notes:
Page 55 – John's decision to come back comes out of nowhere.

Page 78 – This might be good a place to have Bob see Mary with John.

Page 100 – Bob needs to do something more extraordinary to save Mary from John. Also when does Mary realize that John is the wrong guy for her and that Bob is the right guy?

DEVELOPMENT NOTES—DOS & DON'TS

1) Be sure to use present tense.

2) Do not personalize with words like "I think..." or "It seems to me..." or "I find..." rather say "It is..." or "It should be..." etc. "It is more definitive" rather than "I think it is more definitive." Though a neutral voice is better, sometimes you need to use the "royal we"—which is best used when you're representing a consensus of multiple people on a project, i.e., when consolidating the notes from a producer, director, and studio execs use "we believe," "we suggest," etc. If the executive knows the writer, he or she can be more personal and conversational and state things in a first person voice, but the more objective they are, the more useful the notes will be.

3) Be committed to your comments and notes—do not use phrases like: "The story is a *little bit* unfocused," instead use "The story is unfocused...and this is what needs to be done to make it focused." Or change "The character does not *seem* to have a clear throughline" to "The character does not have a clear throughline." Don't be wishy-washy about it—be committed to what you are saying and avoid using ambiguous words.

4) Try to find more descriptive words to use in describing the story, the characters and the affect the screenplay has on the reader. For example, it is too easy to use words like "interesting" when you can find something more descriptive like "compelling," "suspenseful," or "unique," to name a few—Use a thesaurus to expand your use of words in your commentary.

5) When saying something is "underdeveloped"—back it up with what needs to be done to make it more developed and also why you think it is underdeveloped. This is the easiest comment to give, but it is not always the easiest thing to verbally convey how you would fix it.

6) You should also point out what works in the script. It's always good for the writer(s) to know what you liked and what they need not concern themselves with so they can focus on what needs to be done. It's always good to temper criticism with acknowledgement of what's good, e.g., "This is a laugh out loud script with wonderful comedic characters." However, if you put insincere flattery in, the writer will use it to discredit your criticisms. Consistency of your ideas is the thing that makes it useful to writers.

7) Try to think of constructive suggestions to back up your comments and notes on how to fix the problems in order to move the script forward towards a greenlight. It's not enough to tear the script apart. It's not enough to just point out the flaws. The real work comes in the care and thought you use to suggest new ways to make the project better and thus offer ideas towards that end, whether it's digging deeper into the characters to give them more baggage and backstory, or making sure there are no plot holes, or making sure that things are rooted in the reality of that story. Whatever you are trying to fix, the real thought comes in when you are trying to figure out how you can make the story better, deeper, and more cohesive as a tale.

8) Always state "the script" rather than "the writer." William Goldman said that "no one person can hold the equation of movie success in their head"—and similarly no one person can fully keep their eye on the ball in their script without blind spots.

CONCLUSION

The studio executive's life revolves around relationships, networking, finding new stories to make into films, and working with all kinds of talent and production companies in a collaborative way—all with the end result of a "go movie" which will hopefully be successful for the studio. It takes an enormous amount of socializing, reading, knowing how to get along with people and still get your point across, and being able to identify the marketability of each project. Executives must be quick to identify the flaws of a story, and even quicker on how to fix them, all the while doing it with a zeal, encouraging writers and producers to keep coming back for more. To be a good studio executive, you must live, eat, and breathe movies.

EXERCISE 1

Write a talent list for a screenplay. Do it in the format outlined in this chapter. Take a famous screenplay that has already been produced and make an alternative list of talent or take a script you're working on and come up with a talent list for it.

EXERCISE 2

Write development notes on a screenplay. Do it in the format outlined in this chapter. You can find screenplays on the Internet or in bookstores. Even though it may have been produced, pick a movie you had problems with, read the screenplay and do a set of notes, that, in your opinion, would have made the movie better.

5

"Movies Don't Get Made, They're Forced Into Existence"
—Laura Ziskin, Producer

the production company

A production company can be the first rung on the development ladder prior to submitting a project to a studio or independently-financed company, that is, a movie that is financed outside of the studio system. There are hundreds upon hundreds of production companies. Some of these companies are run by writers, actors, or directors; most are run by producers. The major difference between a studio and a production company is that the studio distributes and bankrolls the movies, while the actual production company develops and produces the movies. However, if the production company sets up the movie at a studio, the producer develops the project with the studio's input. Some of these companies have partial financing and need the studio to distribute their films while others have term deals with studios. Some production companies have independent financing though they may sell their finished movies to the studios as acquisitions or negative pickups and use the studio's vast distribution network and marketing departments to help garner a strong release. Today, most major studios have a specialty film arm which buys already-produced movies screened at film festivals or screened at advanced screenings while some have money to buy screenplays and develop them. All have the same intention: to make movies! But in all, they serve as the first step for a writer or a fledgling producer to develop his or her project.

THE PRODUCER

The term "producer" has been misused through the years. Not many people know what a producer does because the credit of producer has often been given out in an arbitrary way. Someone who finds an idea for a film is not necessarily a producer. Someone who is the manager, wife, or brother of the star is not necessarily a producer. A writer who writes the screenplay and receives a producer credit is also not necessarily a producer.

So what does a producer do? A producer usually finds the story first. and options it, meaning they strike an agreement with the writer or writer's representative, or, if it's a book or an article, with the person who owns or controls the rights to that material. They then further develop the material within a limited amount of time; within that time period the producer tries to either obtain financing or set it up at a studio and/or television network.

While the writer births the baby, it is usually the producer who delivers and raises the child. They do this by kneading the story and developing it into a project ready to go out into the world and flourish. From there, the producer sells the material to a studio or obtains financing, followed by overseeing the motion picture through all phases of the production from start to finish. A producer can also be involved in the subsequent marketing strategies of the film. The job of the main producer on a film isn't over until the movie is released. Prior to the movie being made, the producer usually works with the writer to develop the script further, hires a casting director to find the right cast, chooses the director, and troubleshoots any problems throughout the whole production process through the film's release. Sometimes this is done with studio input, sometimes a producer can do it independently.

There are many types of credits a producer may receive; recently the Academy of Motion Picture Arts and Sciences has limited the number of producers who are eligible for their Best Picture award. No more than three producers may be nominated or receive statuettes; if more than three producers are credited on a nominated picture, the Academy Award recipients shall be those three, or fewer, who have performed the major portion of the producing functions and have received a "producer" or "produced by" credit. No other producing credits are eligible. In short, the nominated producers must have fully functioned as producers on the picture.

It is hard to define the roles performed by producers, but with the input of the Producers Guild of America (PGA), the following may be helpful in describing the producer's responsibilities:

- **PRODUCER**—A "produced by" credit is the primary producing credit for all theatrical motion pictures. The producer should have final responsibility for all business and creative aspects of the production of the motion picture. A producer is involved throughout all phases of production from inception to completion. The buck stops here. This is the kingpin.

    In television movies, however, the executive producer performs the same function as a producer does on a theatrical film. It is the primary credit for all movies made-for-television. A producer on a made-for-television movie answers to the executive producer.

- **EXECUTIVE PRODUCER**—Sometimes an executive producer secures an essential and proportionately significant part (no less than 25 percent per the Producers Guild guidelines) of the financing for the motion picture. Sometimes an executive producer has made a significant contribution to the development of the literary property—typically, including the procurement of the underlying rights to the material upon which the motion picture is based. Regardless, the executive producer supports the producer and helps on an "as needed" basis.

    However, the executive producer in television is quite a different position than in a feature film. For example, the executive producer in series television is usually the creator/writer for the series. In fact, most producing credits in series television are given to writers. For movies of the week or made-for-television movies, an executive producer actually serves the same function as a producer does for feature films as stated above, in that they are the ones in charge and oversee the development from beginning through delivery to the network of the movie.

- **LINE PRODUCER**—The line producer hires the below-the-line crew and supervises the day-to-day physical aspects of making a motion picture or television production. The creative decision-making process is reserved for others, except to such extent that the line producer is permitted to participate. The line producer has also been known to receive executive producer or co-producer credit.

- **CO-PRODUCER**—Co-producers are individuals who report directly to the individual(s) receiving "produced by" credit. Many times the co-producer is the line producer and is the person primarily responsible for the logistics of the production, from pre-production through completion of production. Some producers receive co-producer credit in the beginning of their careers or if they perform limited producing duties. Sometimes the unit production manager will receive a co-producer credit. However, this is one of those credits that get arbitrarily thrown in as a bonus in the deal-making process to writers, their managers, actors, and others who are connected but not actually producing the project. This is not to denigrate anyone who receives a co-producer credit because there are some very strong co-producers who absolutely deserve this credit. It should just be noted, once again, that the term producer is not as appreciated as it should be.

- **ASSOCIATE PRODUCER**—An associate producer performs one or more producer functions delegated to him or her by a producer. This credit may also be at the sole discretion of the producer and should be granted only for those individuals who are given significant producing functions.

  However, in series television, associate producers may supervise the post-production of the series.

Now that we have our definition of producer, it is important to note that producers fall into two categories: the studio term deal producer—which has previously been defined—and the independent producer, one without a studio deal who still sells to studios or partners with other production companies to sell their movies to the studios or raise the financing themselves.

THE PRODUCTION COMPANY

So, how does the production company work? Usually, production companies work on a smaller scale than a studio yet use similar procedures. Some production companies have a number of vice presidents of creative affairs, development, and/or production; some have directors of development or creative executives while others only have one creative executive and one assistant. Production companies vary in size (thereby reflecting a creative staff based upon that size). For example, a large production company like Imagine Entertainment will have a much bigger staff than a small production company, which would usually consist of a producer, a development executive, and an assistant. The more projects a producer has in development, the more his or her production company may grow. The more projects that get produced and are successful, the better the chance the production company is given a term deal with a studio. Whether large or small, the job is the same: to find material, oversee its development, sell it to a studio and/or network or obtain independent financing, and to oversee the production and post-production of the movie until delivery to the screen.

THE PRODUCTION COMPANY CREATIVE EXECUTIVE

The difference between a studio executive and a production company executive, once again, varies depending on the size of the production company; their slate might be smaller, requiring smaller staffs, and they service many studios rather than just one. Even though some production companies have a home base or a term deal with a studio, it is usually a first look and, therefore, they are still free to go to other studios to sell their projects when or if their home studio passes. Also, most production companies are both buyers and sellers—that is, they may option and/or purchase material and then sell or set it up at a studio or financing entity—whereas the studio is a buyer only.

Because of the variety of production companies out there, an exec might work for a hyphenate, meaning someone who serves in more than one function, e.g., a writer who also directs, or an actor who produces movies. They may also work strictly for a bona fide producer. While some companies allow for executives to work on their own passion projects, most executives feed the agenda of the company. They must be able to sniff out material that they know their boss will respond to and want to develop. Therefore, they must have great relationships with agents and managers in order to get that material. While some companies allow unsolicited material, most do not. Like the studios, most production companies cannot

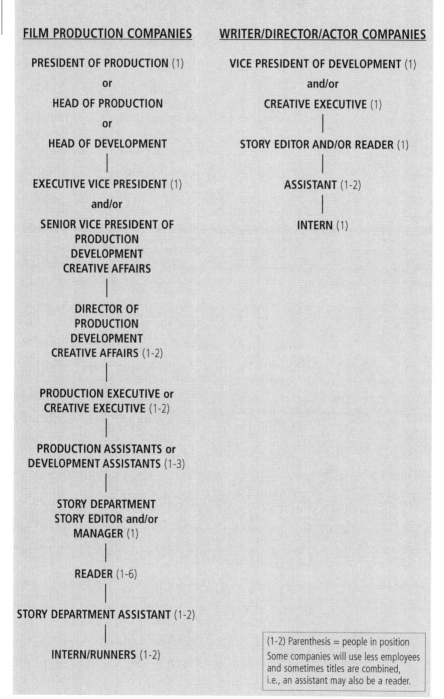

EXECUTIVES AND POSITIONS AT PRODUCTION COMPANIES

FILM PRODUCTION COMPANIES

PRESIDENT OF PRODUCTION (1)

or

HEAD OF PRODUCTION

or

HEAD OF DEVELOPMENT

|

EXECUTIVE VICE PRESIDENT (1)

and/or

SENIOR VICE PRESIDENT OF
PRODUCTION
DEVELOPMENT
CREATIVE AFFAIRS

|

DIRECTOR OF
PRODUCTION
DEVELOPMENT
CREATIVE AFFAIRS (1-2)

|

PRODUCTION EXECUTIVE or
CREATIVE EXECUTIVE (1-2)

|

PRODUCTION ASSISTANTS or
DEVELOPMENT ASSISTANTS (1-3)

|

STORY DEPARTMENT
STORY EDITOR and/or
MANAGER (1)

|

READER (1-6)

|

STORY DEPARTMENT ASSISTANT (1-2)

|

INTERN/RUNNERS (1-2)

WRITER/DIRECTOR/ACTOR COMPANIES

VICE PRESIDENT OF DEVELOPMENT (1)

and/or

CREATIVE EXECUTIVE (1)

|

STORY EDITOR AND/OR READER (1)

|

ASSISTANT (1-2)

|

INTERN (1)

(1-2) Parenthesis = people in position
Some companies will use less employees
and sometimes titles are combined,
i.e., an assistant may also be a reader.

accept any material unless it comes via an agent or an entertainment attorney; if they do accept unsolicited work, they require a signed release form from the writer. This protects the company from future lawsuits claiming that a writer submitted a script that was similar to something produced by that company. The release form indemnifies the production company should they have something comparable in development.

It is up to the creative executive of a production company to network with a variety of people including studio execs, talent such as writers and directors, agents and managers, as well as their counterparts at other production companies in order to stay on top of the latest spec scripts in the marketplace and the hottest new writers being read.

Each production company has a track record of certain types of films they produce. As a production company executive, one needs to have an affinity for the types of movies made by that company. Not to pigeonhole the taste of the company, but for the most part if that production company is known for big action tentpole movies, they are unlikely to produce smaller indie fare. For example, Jerry Bruckheimer produces big studio motion pictures, usually with a lot of action and thrills. He's very, very good at them. That being said, Bruckheimer will, once in awhile, produce smaller, character-driven films such as *Veronica Guerin* (2003) or *Coyote Ugly* (2000). After having so many blockbusters in his stable, he can afford to produce a small passion project. This is rare and not the norm. For the most part, you wouldn't go pitching a small woman's story to a company that produces male-oriented action films. That's not to say that a producer might not want to make something different from what their company is known for, but studios expect a certain kind of movie out of such production companies and they have to keep supplying that pipeline.

Some companies use their clout to get their passion movies made. Tom Cruise, one of the biggest stars today, has a first look deal at Paramount for his production company, Cruise-Wagner Productions (also known as C/W Productions). He'll lend his name to independent projects such as *Narc* (2002) as well as produce *Shattered Glass* (2003) or appear in *Magnolia* (1999), yet he's best known for doing big blockbuster studio films such as *The Last Samurai* (2003) or *Mission Impossible* (1996). Imagine Entertainment has a well-earned reputation for high concept comedies, and while they still do them, the tastes of producers Ron Howard and Brian Grazer have grown into more serious subject matter. The company known for *Liar, Liar* (1997) also produced the Oscar winner, *A Beautiful Mind* (2001). So while we are giving you a certain protocol to follow, it should be noted there are exceptions to every rule. How you find out about these exceptions is usually via networking with fellow executives.

Whether you're a writer submitting material to a production company, seeking an assistant, reader, or executive position, or looking to co-produce with a particular company, it is imperative that you know what these companies are looking for and to whom they are selling. Every year, *Daily Variety* puts out an article called "Facts on Pacts," listing all the current production companies who have term deals with studios. *The Hollywood Creative Directory* (published three times a year and also available online) lists up-to-the-minute deals at studios and TV networks, including their contact information. These are great resources that can be used for readers looking for jobs or writers and producers wanting to submit their material to a studio-based or indie production company, studio, television production company, or television network.

The production company executive services the company for which he or she works. To that end, creative executives try to make sure they are in the forefront of receiving the latest specs from agents and managers. They work with writers to develop their material and then try to sell it to a studio or attach talent in what is called "packaging." Packaging is when one or more pieces of talent or elements (e.g., an actor or director) are attached to the project prior to studio submission or before obtaining financing from other sources.

In many ways, the production company executive works in much the same way as a studio creative executive in that they are out there finding material, developing it, selling it, and, hopefully, making it. The difference is that a studio creative exec works for one studio who is the buyer while a production company exec can buy or option material, yet is not usually limited to just one studio to set it up. The production company executive has many options and must strategize about how to best service the material, the right studio or company to go to, and determine the best way to sell it. The production company executive shepherds the project on behalf of the company and is the conduit to the studio. While answering to his boss—the producer—the production company executive may offer suggestions on how to fix a problem with the script, do explicit notes, and work with writers. They represent the producer when he or she cannot be at a meeting. It is important for a creative executive at a production company to realize they are the face of their company to the outside world. They represent their boss' taste and serve as unofficial PR people for their companies. By bringing the production company to the forefront and networking with other execs, agents, and managers, they will be in line for better material and projects. If the company has a track record, the executive has an easier time in garnering good material and setting up projects because the company is already respected. On the smaller side, a production company executive working for a fledgling company or newer producer has a great opportunity to raise that company up in the eyes of the industry.

THE DEVELOPMENT ASSISTANT

A development assistant is usually part administrative and part development executive. They read scripts, write coverage (much like the story analyst at a studio), and attend creative meetings. They are responsible for assisting the production company creative executive in any way deemed necessary. Sometimes they will provide secretarial duties by setting up lunches and meetings for the creative executive. Other times they will be privy to negotiations and meetings with writers. Eager assistants network with other assistants at agencies, studios, and production companies while attending parties specifically for assistants, which is the latest craze—assistants helping assistants! They may attend film school screenings of student short films and track screenwriting competitions in the hope of finding the next great talent. Becoming a development assistant is a terrific way to move up into a development executive job. Never underestimate these assistants. They may have the power to hire you a few years down the line!

DEVELOPMENT INTERNS

Most production companies use interns and most studios have summer internship programs. An intern is usually a person or student who wants to gain on-the-job experience working for a production company. Most internships are credit-based, in that the intern earns college credit for their time on the job, and are usually unpaid. However, it is a great way for a person to learn the inner workings of a company and many interns get hired by these companies after they have proven themselves on the job. Countless success stories have been told by executives and presidents of studios and production companies who started out as interns. An intern might run errands for the company, deliver and pick up scripts, read material, and even learn to do coverage. Depending on the production company, interns may also be included in development or creative meetings. Most execs and producers want to hear outside opinions. It keeps things fresh. Some companies may use interns strictly as gophers. Even this has its merits because you get to know the players involved and soak up much information. Depending on your personality, an internship is a great way to get your foot in the door. It can be a stepping-stone towards becoming a full-time employee and moving up the ladder.

READERS

Production companies might employ freelance readers. Most, however, use someone in-house, such as the development assistant or possibly an intern, to read submissions. To be a freelance reader you do not have to be part of the union. A good way to ingratiate yourself with production companies (especially smaller ones) is to send a sample coverage to show your work and then offer a good introductory rate, sometimes free for the experience, on the first coverage done for the company. If they like your work and can afford freelance readers, you may get some steady work. Though some companies may have their own format for coverage, most use a format similar to that of the studios. Some may eliminate the box scores, some may require a shorter synopsis—almost all require a logline and comments.

THE PROCESS OF SUBMITTING TO A PRODUCTION COMPANY

What happens to a screenplay when it's submitted to a production company? It generally follows the same path as a studio submission, just to a lesser degree. Depending on the size of the production company, there may be fewer reports but there is always coverage. The vice president or director of development may read the script themselves or hand it to a reader for coverage. The creative executive will then decide whether to present it to his or her boss to see if there's interest in the project. Sometimes their boss will read it right away or overnight. Usually after everyone's on board to move forward with the project, there is a meeting to discuss the merits of the script and decide whether to option the project out of a discretionary fund if the production company has a term deal at a studio (or sometimes out of the production company's own pocket), or to get permission from the writer or his representative to take it into studios. If the studio likes the project, they will buy it or option it on behalf of that production company. The reason why a company may want to option it prior to submitting it to a studio is to take it off the market to prevent other production companies from competing for it, and/or to develop it further and get it into shape before the studio sees it, with the hope of making it more palatable for a sale to the studio. If a production company does not have a studio deal, the process is still the same with the exception that they can submit it to any studio first or even go to multiple studios at the same time—hopefully eliciting some competition, which in turn can heat up the prospect of a sale.

A DAY IN THE LIFE OF A PRODUCTION COMPANY CREATIVE EXECUTIVE

Much like the studio executive, the day usually begins for a creative or development executive, whether a VP or a director of development/production, with a breakfast meeting. The exec may meet with an agent, manager, or other production company executives, usually with the goal of finding new material, learning about new writers or directors, or submitting material to partner with other production companies. When the executive arrives at the office he or she might discuss, with the development assistant or other company creative execs, scripts that were read the night before and decide whether or not to go after a spec that may be on the market. Then it's time to call or e-mail other production company executives to find out what's going on in the marketplace that day or follow the input on a tracking board. Any submissions that come in are logged in by the development assistant and placed into priority piles. If the company has a project in production, there may be dailies to watch or discussions on how the shoot is going. If a project is in development, there may be meetings with the writer to discuss notes or talk with the studio executive about how the project is moving along and what needs to be done. There may be pitch meetings with writers and/or other producers. When lunchtime comes around, you can bet there will be another opportunity to network with a studio executive or other producers, all with an eye toward buying and selling stories. After lunch, an executive may have production meetings, more pitch meetings, or what are called generals or meet-and-greet meetings. These are meetings usually set up after an executive has a read a spec script and liked it enough to take a general meeting with the writer who wrote it. Sometimes the executive has open writing assignments to fill and is busily reading writing samples sent in from various agents. The executive will create a talent list for that open writing assignment and find out availabilities of the writers (usually starting with the top A+ writers). This is done in association with the studio executive, with an eye toward compiling a list of writers who are approved by the studio. Then it's presented to the boss and phone calls are made to determine whether or not the writer will be interested in the project and the writer's availability. However, there have been many times when a brand new writer has been hired just because the company liked a recent spec by that writer.

The executive's day doesn't end at 6:00 PM. In fact, they stay as late as necessary to complete their day's work or go to an industry-related dinner engagement, or attend a premiere or screening. Usually these events are related to their agenda of networking with people in the industry who can bring them new material, meeting new talent such as writers and directors, or conferring with colleagues. Do they sleep? Only sometimes...as there's usually a spec script or two to read at night—that's not counting a weekend read of a bunch of scripts.

As you've probably figured out, reading is the backbone of most of the creative jobs in the industry. You can't be a studio creative executive, story analyst/reader, production company creative executive, producer, actor, writer, or director without reading lots and lots of screenplays.

WORKING WITH THE STUDIO

If a production company does not have a term deal with a studio, the producer and creative executive at the production company need to cultivate relationships with one or more executives at each of the studios. To do this, it's best to be recommended to that executive by someone who already has a relationship with them. An agent or manager can be very helpful in making that introduction, as can a fellow producer or development executive. If the production company has a produced credit, the producer or creative executive can use that as a way of getting in the door to pitch or submit other projects. Once inside, it is important to find out the kinds of projects the studio may be looking for or if they are looking for something for a particular actor or director. Don't pitch them something they've said they are not in the market for! Give them a logline to whet their appetite and then maybe they will be open to receiving the script. They may require you to sign a release form, but usually producers are able to submit projects without this. Writers, on the other hand, must always sign a release form if they are submitting without benefit of representation by an agent or a lawyer, and even then only if the executive is open to what is called unsolicited material, meaning the material is coming in without representation. When the studio receives the script, the procedure works as already described in Chapter 3—*The Story Department.*

If the studio buys or options the script, they begin working with the producer and production company executive allowing either the original writer to rewrite the existing script (incorporating studio notes) or finding a new writer to do the rewrite, attaching elements, etc.—all trying to move the film into production.

Sometimes a production company may team up with another production company prior to going into a studio with a project. An actor or a director's company might be beneficial for the project and carry more clout, upping the studio's interest. Generally, an executive will contact his counterpart at another production company and try and get that person to read the script. If the other executive likes it, he may have total autonomy or have to get it approved by the head of the company, usually a partner to the talent, or possibly the talent themselves. Once this is done, the project may be ready to go out to the studios as a package and the process starts within the studio system all over again.

MINI-MAJOR STUDIOS

Within the studio system, there lies another kind of studio that is called a "mini-major." These studios are independently financed production companies that have signed distribution and/or co-production deals with one of the major studios. They should be counted as separate from their parent studio as they have total autonomy to develop and finance motion pictures. The difference is that they already have in place the where-with-all to distribute through a major studio. Most have output deals with major studios such as Fox, Sony, Disney, and Warner Bros. All are considered "buyers" just like the major studios.

GOING THE INDIE ROUTE

Many production companies raise their own financing on a per film basis. But what does it take to do this? First off, above all, you need a distinctive story and a good script.

- One that will attract talent, i.e., a director or actors.
- One that will be commercial enough (not necessarily in the high-concept studio sense) to garner distribution and hence have a release in theatres.
- One that will appeal to audiences in territories around the globe including Europe, Asia, and South America.
- One that could be licensed for cable television.
- One that might have a strong DVD/video shelf life.

Second, an indie producer will often take a screenplay and try to attach an element that is attractive to investors or financing companies.

The talent attached will greatly affect the interest of investors. There are some tools out there that can aid in mapping this often complex, difficult process. *The Ulmer Scale*, which has not been updated in recent years, was the film industry's premier series of power bases for tracking, measuring, and ranking the star power of actors and directors worldwide. The higher the score, the more probable financing can be obtained. Another research tool is *The Hollywood Reporter*'s *Star Power*® and *Director Power*® global bankability surveys. The reports, which *THR* has conducted at different times during the past decade or so (the last one was done in 2002), take a look at the ability of an individual (actor or director) to obtain financing for a feature film based upon various criteria and then sending a ballot to industry voters worldwide in the key areas of production, financing, marketing people, as well as executives at the studios and independent arenas. The most recent *Star Power*® looked at 1,100-plus actors, while the most recent *Director Power*® ranked 800-plus helmers. For *Star Power*®, they are asked to rank actors/actresses in one of five categories:

- Maximum Star Power—This is the crème de la crème in terms of worldwide audience following and bankability. They can guarantee financing even reading the phone book. They ensure wide releases and are willing to promote the film. Even bad press can rarely harm their star power appeal.
- Strong Star Power—One rung below Maximum, these actors can often but not always open a film on the strength of their name alone. Recent boxoffice success is a key indicator of their star power. They can also ensure major studio and, definitely, independent distribution.
- Moderate Star Power—These actors have an important impact on the films they make, but the impact is more of a contributory nature rather than dominant. They strengthen a package but do not dominate it. They usually can't open a film alone, but their name on the film is an important contribution. They can, also, be valuable to specific territories, pay, video, and free TV rights deals.
- Minimum Star Power—These actors are not likely to affect major decisions regarding financing or distribution. However, these people do help with the overall strength of the film as casting choices in addition to the above Star Power.
- No Star Power—These actors are not likely to make a difference on how well a film does. It doesn't mean they give poor performances, rather it means any number of actors could be cast in these roles and it would make no impact on the film's performance.

For *Director Power*®, directors are ranked by criteria similar to what's used for the actors list in regards to bankability. Agents *do not* get to vote on this, as it would stack the deck in favor of their clientele. This is strictly for global film execs who are the key people in their fields. *Star Power*® offers a snapshot or blueprint that constantly changes with the advent of new, up-and-coming stars, and is used as one element in the process of understanding the global elements from a financing and marketing perspective.

There is a search engine on *The Hollywood Reporter's* Web site that allows subscribers a per access fee to search their database. A copy of the full report is also available to non-subscribers and subscribers for a fee. With *Star Power*® and *Director Power*®, *The Hollywood Reporter* sees it as an opportunity for an end-user to not only look at the U.S., but "also to think globally and act globally."

It is not always easy to attach that element and it's a long arduous process to get agents and managers to read the material and then forward to their clients a project that has no financing attached yet. However, actors, in particular, are always hungry for good roles and sometimes a producer can entice a well-known talent with a really well-written character. Actors have been known to work in low budget films for scale, meaning union minimum wage; for a piece of the backend, which means a percentage of profits; or because the role is something not usually offered to them in the studio system and it gives them an opportunity to grow. Many have been rewarded for this career move by the Academy of Motion Picture Arts and Sciences.

The things you need to present to a financing company are:
- A great script
- A letter of intent from an actor and/or director (or both)
- A budget
- The producer's bio

While there may be more things to consider, these are the key components. Getting financing does not preclude developing the script further. Talent may require a rewrite. Financing companies may also request further development of the material. There are many pieces to the puzzle when going the indie route, but when a movie gets made there can be great satisfaction having done it on your own.

CONCLUSION

A production company has many options to choose from when developing a screenplay. Deciding where they are going to take the script, if they are going to attach elements, and whether it's a studio or an independent film are all part of a strategy formulated for each individual project.

Producers wear many hats as they struggle to make a movie. They have a hand in every aspect of the journey, from the sale through the development, from the production all the way through delivery of the completed film. They are jugglers—keeping on top of who's who at the studios, what they are looking for, and then acquiring, selling, and eventually producing motion pictures.

The creative executive's job at a production company mirrors a lot of what the studio creative executive does. However, unlike the studio executive, they must know how to sell the material and have more flexibility in choosing where to sell it. Like the studio executive, the creative executive at a production company must network with agents, managers, studio executives, and other production company executives while keeping abreast of the latest talent, all in search of optioning fresh material and either setting it up at a studio or network, or obtaining financing for the production company to produce the motion picture independently. They must service whoever is running the company whether a producer, an actor, a director, or a writer, and must be on the same wavelength. They must learn to second guess their boss' taste in material and seek what the producer is looking for, sometimes at the expense of what they may personally appreciate.

If you have learned one thing so far, it should be that relationships and networking are the key to success in this business. As a reader, a studio executive, or a production company executive, even as an assistant or development assistant, the more people you meet and share information with, the more opportunities will come your way.

EXERCISE

Pick a genre or script and then create a potential list of submissions to production companies in which the genre might be a good fit.

Edgar Allan Poe — the first guy to package his clients

LOOK. YOU WANT THE PiT, AND YOU'LL GET THE PiT, BUT YOU HAVE TO TAKE THE PENDULUM, TOO!

oh. ok.

6

"The Three Ss: Sign, Serve, and Sell"

agents & managers and the deal

Literary agents are necessary for writers, but can be very helpful to studio and production company executives as well. An agent's job is to sell his clients' stories, elevate their sales, expose their work, and get them work on open writing assignments.

Agents can represent all kinds of talent, including actors, producers, writers, directors, novelists as well as below-the-line talent (cinematographers, film editors, production designers, etc.). Agencies have many departments—categorized as motion picture literary, television literary, talent, commercials, packaging, and, sometimes, new media. Each department has its own separate stable of agents working within the parameters of their own group. Sometimes the departments cross over, but most of the time a client has a team of agents from each department, particularly at the larger agencies such as CAA, William Morris, and ICM. The bigger agencies are able to package projects more easily because they have large rosters of talent, while the smaller agencies focus more heavily on career development and day-to-day jobs for their writers. Which is better? It depends on where the writer is in his or her career. An agent is only as good as the jobs he gets his clients.

LITERARY AGENTS VS. LITERARY MANAGERS

Years ago, if you had a good agent there was no need for a manager. In today's world, where a number of agencies have merged with each other and the client rosters have grown enormously, it has become increasingly necessary for a writer to have both a manager and an agent. A manager tends to focus on the writer's career as a whole, whereas some agents are "bookers," meaning they are only interested in booking the job and not necessarily what the job will do for the career. Also, at a big agency, there is a tendency for agents to lose interest in the client if the client isn't actively selling screenplays or booking the open writing assignments. Ideally, a manager will not lose interest and is in it for the long-term with his clients. There are, however, some agents who serve their clients in a similar capacity as a manager, in that they like to develop and guide careers. In these cases, it may not be necessary to have a manager.

Some of the primary differences between an agent and a manager in Hollywood are that an agent must be franchised by the state of California and must abide by certain laws and regulations. For example, an agent cannot demand more than a 10 percent commission from his or her clients. Also, agents cannot produce movies. Agencies have to be signatory to the Writers Guild of America (WGA), which means they must abide by the Minimum Basic Agreement (MBA) as negotiated between the producers (actually the studios) and the WGA. An agent negotiates contracts and submits their client's material in order to get them jobs. They also orchestrate spec script sales and live by the *Three Ss*: SIGN, SERVE, and SELL!

Managers, however, are not regulated by the state. They can charge anything they want (though the norm is usually 10-15 percent). They are not governed by any laws or regulations as of yet, though there is protocol. Managers may develop projects with their clients and produce them. Legally, however, they *cannot negotiate* deals on behalf of their clients. Only lawyers or agents can negotiate the deal (but may do so with the manager's input). Legally, a manager cannot submit material to procure employment for their clients. An agent does this. However, a manager can submit a project as a producer for consideration at a production company, studio, or network. Managers usually have fewer clients than agents so they have more time to assist in long-range goals in helping to develop the overall career of their clients.

There is an advantage to obtaining a manager vs. an agent for first time writers. A manager is someone who takes extra time to understand the individual client's talent and needs, both short-term and long-term, whereas an agent might be more focused on the client's current popularity and how much money might be generated from that client. Managers make sure they are known in town and see themselves as complements to agents. They help decide who is the best agent for their client and form an overall plan and strategy for the spec screenplay and the client's career along with the agent. Basically, it's about putting the right team together.

Getting a good agent or manager may not be easy. The WGA offers a list on their Web site of signatory agencies. Sending query letters may get attention but referral is the best way to getting representation. A student film or winning a screenwriting competition will also get noticed by an agent or a manager. Perseverance and getting your work out there is the best calling card.

ENTERTAINMENT ATTORNEYS

Entertainment attorneys look over deals and correct, or redline, the legalese to favor and protect their clients. Writers and other talent will sometimes bypass using an agent and instead use lawyers to negotiate their deals while having managers to help steer their careers. However, it is important to put a strong team together and having a good agent, manager, and a lawyer will only help the client in the long run (though it will cost them more). Entertainment attorneys work in tandem with the agent and manager. If not on an hourly fee, they normally charge clients 5 percent commission, though some have been known to charge up to 10 percent if they are solely negotiating the deals. Like managers, attorneys are prohibited from acting as agents in procuring employment for their client. This does not, however, preclude them from sending material to other production companies, clients, or financing entities in order to facilitate a package and put a movie together. Attorneys can also handle contract disputes and litigation. While they are not usually involved in the development of a screenplay, they can be very influential in putting the pieces together and negotiating deals on behalf of the writer, the producer, and the director.

FINDING TALENT

Like creative executives, agents and managers attend film festivals, student and short film presentations, theatre and staged play readings, and stay on top of screenwriting competitions to discover new talent. They find talent via referrals from other talent, producers, and executives. Sometimes they may look at a cold query letter and send a writer's release form for the writer to sign and return with their material to be read. But most agencies do not accept unsolicited material. Internet screenwriting Web sites offer exposure for winning screenplay competitions which some agents scour for up-and-coming talent. The new wave of speed-pitching and pitch fests have helped numerous writers expose themselves and their work to production companies and agencies that wouldn't normally accept unsolicited material. Everyone is hungry for a good script and we'd all like to believe that a good script will get noticed.

WORKING WITH THE STUDIO

Literary agents and managers network with studio executives to find out what type of material the studios are looking to purchase. From the larger agencies, agents may attend special luncheons with the studio creative staff that may include the president of production. Here they share information in order to do business together. Most agencies assign some of their agents to cover a studio. This means that the agents are assigned to specific studios to find out what open writing and directing assignments are available as well as specific talent needed for projects. These agents visit their appointed studios a few times a month in what are generally called "walk throughs." If the studio is looking for a specific genre film or a film for an actor with whom they have an existing committed deal, the agent will make note of it to bring back to his agency and present it at their staff meetings where all the agents in that department will then discuss who and what to submit to that particular studio. When an agency signs a new client, that client will be introduced to the studio and production company executives. This can be done in many ways. If it's a director, an agent might send the director's reel or set up a screening of his latest film. If it's a writer, an agent might go out with a big spec script throughout the town and create a buzz, developing an avenue to set up a lot of pitch meetings or get the writer considered for open writing assignments.

Agents and managers give writers credibility and often decide which companies are best for a writer's project. They set up meetings for their clients to meet with creative executives and producers (sometimes referred to as "water" meetings—because of the amount of bottled water offered and consumed at these meetings. We've always said that Hollywood keeps the designer water companies in business!). Even so, an agent and manager's effectiveness is only as good as the talent's ability to convince the creative powers that be that they are the ones to be hired for the project and therefore be the "deal closer."

AGENCY STORY DEPARTMENTS

Agencies come in all shapes and sizes, from the large conglomerates to what we call "boutique" or smaller agencies. Some agents read everything themselves or have their assistants screen the material first and will read it if recommended. Most agencies have their own story departments, employing both a story editor and non-union readers. Their readers evaluate material with an eye towards whether the writer is strong enough to become a potential client, or whether the material itself is suitable for certain talent represented by the agency. With so many internal projects submitted from their clients, agents are harder on material submitted from outside sources.

Generally, the larger agencies employ ten to twelve freelance readers. Scripts are submitted to the agency story department by an agent's office solely for coverage. Much like the studio story department, the screenplays are then logged in and assigned a reader. Coverage consists of concept, synopsis, and evaluation. The difference is that agency coverage may include a casting breakdown of the roles, for those agencies that represent actors. Also unlike studio coverage, because an agency is not buying the material, "consider" is a word used more often than at a studio or production company. The material is filtered through their system hoping to find that one role which can elevate their clients, let alone sign a brilliant new writer.

Once the reading turnaround period is decided, i.e., same-day, overnight, or one-week, the reader hands in the coverage, which is sent via e-mail to the requesting agent. That piece of coverage is now available for all agents to access via a vast database system. Based upon that coverage, an agent will decide whether to take the material and writer on as a client. Sometimes this is done by committee, in which case more than one agent has to vote in order to sign a new client.

While a lot goes into deciding which clients to sign and what material to go out with, there is an unwritten checklist that helps story editors, readers, and agents make these decisions:

- If they're looking at material for a star, writer, or director client, they ask themselves, "Think not what the client does for the script, but what the script does for the client!"
- Does the script offer roles certain to attract top talent?
- Does the script have a wildly compelling premise?
- Does the script support itself with a spectacular execution?
- Does the script have something important to say and deliver the dramatic goods?
- Is it a monster vehicle, meaning is it a great role for a big star?
- Is there a movie-stealing supporting role that could make a client a star, or might it be Oscar bait for an established client?

If a screenplay has some of these characteristics, it may be considered by an agency. If not, it may get a pass.

THE SPEC SALE—A WEEK IN THE LIFE OF A SPEC SCRIPT

"It only takes one to make a sale and two to make a bidding war!"

Much has been written about the spec screenplay sale. It is not as easy as it looks and is getting harder every day. It is very rare that it happens overnight, but some still happen within days or just a week. However, spec scripts continue to be used to help expose writers, as well as try and get a fast sale—sometimes for a lot of money. The following will give a good idea of what exactly happens when a spec screenplay hits the marketplace and how the process plays out.

Agents/Managers and Notes

Most agents will work with writers to make sure the script is in the best possible condition prior to sending it out to the town. Some writers have been known to write several drafts of a screenplay, sometimes even four or five, before their agent or manager feels it's ready to be seen. A good agent or manager will take the time and not rush the process just to get a script out to the town. It's important for a writer to realize that the agent, as well as the manager, wants to make a sale just as much as the writer does, and, therefore, wants the writer to cross every "t" and dot every "i" as well as develop the story to its fullest.

There are, of course, some agents who do nothing more than fling a script out into the marketplace and hope for a sale. Sometimes it's just safety in numbers—the more product out there, the better the chance of at least one sale. But, there are quite a few agents who act in a managerial way, controlling the script and where it goes, guiding a client's career, and doing what's best and the most beneficial for both project and client.

Agents and managers work together in many different capacities. An agent might rely on a manager to work with the writer first to get the script up to speed before they become involved with it and offer their notes. They should become a team as they strategize where the script should be placed and how to create the buzz. Sometimes this buzz can be created by the use of tracking boards, sometimes it's just mentioning the screenplay to the right people, knowing they will be sharing that information with others, stating good things about the script...thus a buzz is created. All this is done with the agent controlling the strings.

Once an agent feels the screenplay is ready to be seen, he or she will brainstorm and create a huge list of potential targets—places where the writer has the biggest fans, places where the project might be a good fit, and possibly new production companies to introduce the writer. Going out with a spec script today is not as easy as it was five or ten years ago. Back then, studios spent way too much money and got burned on huge sales that either never got made or bombed in the theatres. Thus, while the job of the agent is to sell their client's material, it is also important to utilize the spec process to introduce or re-introduce a client to the town. Once the agent creates this huge submission list, he or she will narrow it down to twenty to forty production companies. Where else but Hollywood can you get twenty or more companies to do anything overnight? Only with a spec script going out wide to the town can this be accomplished. The goal of going out with a spec script is not just to sell it—while that's a very important part of it—but the real goal is to get the writer a job. Not only are production companies and studio executives reading for new projects, they are also reading to fill open writing assignments. The list is created and now the agent deals with the various production companies, usually planning on Tuesday or Wednesday for the screenplay to hit the town.

Production Companies and Agents

It is up to the agent to whet the appetite of production company executives who have term deals at the studios. Some agents will give an advantage to some of those companies by placing them in first position, so if they like the script, they have the right to take it into their studio first. However, most do not like to assign territories—meaning studios. Sometimes an agent will go to three companies who have a deal at one studio and then decide the next day, if those companies like the material, which one of them will get their home studio. Production companies without studio deals have to convince agents to let them take the spec script into a studio even though they are without a term deal there. An agent might still let one of those companies have a territory because of the relationship the producer has with a particular studio. It's like a chess game, full of strategy, placement, and the occasional sneak attack. Most agents choose to go out with a spec on a Tuesday.

Tuesday:

Once the list of production companies have been called, they'll send messengers to pick up the scripts from the agencies and read them overnight. Sometimes, screenplays are sent in PDF files via e-mail. It is up to the production company executive or producer to call the agent back after reading the screenplay as soon as possible in order to try and convince them that they are the right company to submit the material to their home studio. The agent plays the strategy of determining who is best for the screenplay and which executive the company plans to submit it to. It's very important to make sure the studio executive has an affinity for the kind of material submitted and who might have hired the writer in the past and now needs to be rewarded.

Meanwhile, it would be most improbable that the information about that particular script, writer, and agent has not hit the tracking boards. This can add to the buzz already created and the agent may receive more phone calls from creative executives not on the original list who now want to read the script. At this point, the agent will decide whether to accommodate those extra production companies or not.

Wednesday:

By noon, hopefully, the agent is barraged with phone calls from production company executives clamoring to take the material into their studio. An agent might ask the executive—who are their three strongest territories? Based upon that, along with the other criteria above, the decision is made as to who is taking the screenplay into what studio. It is important for most agents to have many different producers submit to the various studios rather than just one submitting to all of them. This is because it shows that more than one company is interested, which helps to create the heat that, with any luck, will inspire a studio to act fast and take the project off the market. Alternatively, an agent might package a film with a particular production company first and allow that company to go out to the studios with the project solo, but that's only if it has been decided beforehand and the parties have agreed to go directly to the studios.

This can happen for many reasons:
- The writer has a relationship with that production company.
- The company has strong relationships at the studios.
- The company has their own money—possibly they've optioned the material out of their own funds or can bring financing to the table which will entice a studio.

The process for the latter is somewhat the same except the production company is taking it into the studios with the input of the agent.

Once those production companies are singled out to submit to their studio, it is a waiting game. Some studios may not be covered—meaning no production company has stepped up to the plate to take the project into that particular studio. The agent will then hand off that territory to another production company who has shown enthusiasm for the material and will champion it. Some production companies will receive more than one territory. Again, it's like a puzzle and the agent must dole out the pieces carefully in order to complete the process and win the game. If a company passes, the agent will ask them to keep it quiet in order for the submission process to play out and not have others influenced by any negativity.

Thursday:

Hopefully before the weekend, a studio will pick up the project and start negotiations with the agent and production company. Sometimes, a studio will wait it out, meaning they will see if someone else bids on it and if not, they will come in and offer a lower sum of money for the project. Most times, the script doesn't sell.

If a studio passes, the agent will ask for discretion and ask them to keep it quiet till they have an answer from all the other studios. If a studio makes an offer, the agent will inform the other production companies who still have outstanding submissions at other studios, and try to play one against the other to get answers and raise the bidding. Sometimes a studio will offer a high enough bid and tell the agent to take the material off the table—meaning out of contention—while they complete the deal. That can be a great scenario because the studio will know they have to pay more if they take it off the marketplace.

Friday:

The studios are slow to make an offer. They may need to have other executives or the head of production read it. So, the deal and process of the sale continues into the weekend—where studios may put it on the weekend read for discussion in Monday morning's staff meeting. The writer is biting his or her nails having to go through a weekend not knowing and the agent and manager go out and drink...separately. All of them console each other as the weekend takes forever to end.

Monday:

Offers are being made. Everyone is feeling really good now. A business affairs executive calls the agent and starts to negotiate. The studio will want to know what the writer has done before, what kind of money he or she has received in the past (their quote), and so forth. If the writer has no credits, they will low ball the deal, but it is up to the agent to put pressure on the studio and try to drive the price up. If there is no other studio bidding, the agent might use humor or even guilt to get what they want. One agent told us that they got the price up by telling the business affairs exec that the writer was having a baby. Another agent cajoled another business affairs exec by screaming, "It's not your money!" Whatever works as long as there's a deal on the table.

If there is no deal on the table, hopefully the spec screenplay will serve as a great writing sample for the writer, and the agent will get him lots of meetings for open writing assignments based upon that script.

It is true that in these economic and belt-tightening times, the spec sale frenzy is not what it once was. Some agents still use this method to create heat on a project. Today, most agents are more careful when submitting material. Studios expect scripts to be perfect (even though once they put them into development, they will rewrite and rewrite them again and again). So an agent today must carefully craft a strategy that will not kill the project. They do this by packaging material with talent: directors and/or actors. One agent told us that they don't go out to thirty producers like they used to. Instead, they limit their submissions to ten or twenty production companies and even then, they go out with only a few one week and a few the next week, asking the prospective buyer to let them know what they think and if they want to get involved with the project and help them put it together before submitting to a studio or a financing entity. Even the larger agencies are more open to entertaining a script without an offer attached if the producer bringing it in has a track record. A producer can be helpful, utilizing their contacts with talent and other agencies to assemble a package that will entice a studio to step up to the plate and put the screenplay into development or fast track it for production.

The Deal

The deal can be many things. It can be an option in which the studio does not own the script but pays money for a limited amount of time to develop the material. Eventually an option may lead to the studio buying it completely. The script might be purchased outright, meaning the studio ponies up the money to buy the screenplay, owning it in perpetuity. The deal might offer the writer one rewrite and a polish or have other built-in rewrites all paid in what are called steps, either committed or optional— the writer gets paid after each step of the way and can be cut off after an optional step, should the studio want to hire someone else. However, the Writers Guild of America states that a screenplay can revert back to the writer five years from the date of the original sale or the original writer's services (whichever is later) within a two-year reacquisition period. This is like a turnaround for the writer, meaning that the writer has the opportunity to buy back his rights from the studio within that two-year reacquisition period. If the script is optioned and the option not renewed, the script reverts back to the writer automatically, though there may be turnaround costs (whatever the studio initially forked out for the re-written screenplay, plus interest), which would have to be repaid should the screenplay be set up elsewhere. For more specific information on this, the WGA can be very helpful. Agents and entertainment attorneys are getting more and more creative these days in order to get their writers paid more and keep them attached to projects as long as possible.

The agent or entertainment attorney deals with studio business affairs executives. "Business affairs" negotiates the deal on behalf of the studio while studio "legal affairs" prepares the actual contracts and documents. Legal affairs answers to business affairs. The business affairs executive answers to the head of production. They will constantly go back and forth with the talent's representation and report to the studio creative executives responsible for bringing in the project the different points of the deal. Usually the creative executive in charge of the project will have certain parameters to work within—the ceiling price (the highest amount the studio or production company will pay), steps (how many rewrites and polishes), bonuses (if it goes to production or if a writer gets sole writing credit, there may be built-in bonuses negotiated), etc. Sometimes, if a deal reaches beyond the agreed parameters set by the head of production, the studio creative executive might have to approach the head of production again to see if they will approve anything beyond what was already agreed and discussed. In the end, the studio creative executive will sign off on the deal, meaning they approve it, and the business affairs executive will close the deal with the agent and hand it over to legal affairs to memorialize the deal on paper.

Once the deal is made, the real work starts: development, development, development. Rewrite, rewrite, rewrite. And if all goes well...greenlight, greenlight, greenlight! Or if not, turnaround, turnaround, turnaround...sob, sob, sob.

CONCLUSION

A good agent or manager is someone with clout, who is well-connected, can get studio executives and producers on the phone, and have material get the attention of senior executives. Good agents and managers are aggressive in selling new clients and know the spec market, having made current deals at studios and production companies. They should be able to provide intelligent notes on material before sending it out to see if it "sticks." Good agents and managers give feedback on what is working and what is not working in a screenplay. In addition, they should be able to advise their client to say "no" to an open writing assignment, a project that may not further the writer's career, or a script that is just plain bad. Writers shouldn't count on their agents and managers for all their work. They, too, need to be out there networking and utilizing their own contacts with film professionals. Solid writing will get attention—however, it has to be read first!

Whether a writer is a signed client or a hip pocket client (meaning they are represented without paperwork or an agent or manager might be testing the waters to see what the response is to that client before signing them), it is important to get exposure. An agent and manager can be essential keys to a writing, directing, or an acting career.

Sample Release Form

WRITER'S RELEASE FORM

Ms. Rona Edwards
Ms. Monika Skerbelis
EDWARDS SKERBELIS ENTERTAINMENT
264 S. La Cienega Blvd., Suite 1052
Beverly Hills, CA 90211

Dear Ms. Edwards and Ms. Skerbelis,

I am submitting to you today the following described materials (the "Property"):

_____

_____

(Give a complete description of the Property you are submitting—including title, page count, whether it's a screenplay, treatment, etc., and the writer's name—and attach the materials to this Release.)

I request that you examine the Property with a view to using them as the basis for all or part of a television program or feature film. You are under no obligation to read or use the Property, nor are you under any obligation to pay me or compensate me in any way for submitting them to you.

I recognize that other persons including your own employees may have submitted to you or made public or may hereafter originate and submit to you or make public materials similar or identical to the Property which you may then have the right to use. I understand that I will not be entitled to any compensation because of use by you of any such other similar or identical materials. I agree that nothing in this Release shall be deemed to create a confidential relationship between you and me or shall place you in a position different from that of a member of the general public with respect to the use of the Property. In no event shall I be entitled to, nor shall I demand, any compensation or any legal or equitable remedy other than the fair market value of the Property at the time of this submission to you.

I represent and warrant that I am the sole owner and author of the Property, that they are original with me and that I have the exclusive right to submit them to you upon the terms and conditions of this letter. I retain all rights to submit the Property or any similar materials to persons other than you.

I have retained a copy of the Property, and you need not return the attached materials to me. If you decide not to use them, you do not have to tell me the reasons for your rejection. If you ask me to develop the Property or if you make me an offer to purchase the Property, and we do not come to an agreement, your making such a request or offer will not be deemed to mean that you thought the Property was original or novel or that you thought I was the first person to submit it to you.

The words "you" or "your" in this release refer to EDWARDS SKERBELIS ENTERTAINMENT and its officers, agents, employees, affiliated companies, licensees, successors and assigns. If the Property is submitted by more than one person or by a firm, corporation or other entity, the words "I", "my" or "me" shall refer to all such persons, firms, corporations or other entities, and this release will be binding jointly and severally upon all such persons, firms, corporations or other entities.

I HAVE READ THIS RELEASE CAREFULLY AND I UNDERSTAND ITS CONTENTS. No representations have been made to me other than those set forth in this Release and this Release states our entire understanding with references to the Property.

I understand that if I make any modification or change in the provisions of this Release and send you the Property, the modification or change made by me shall be void and of no effect and shall not be binding upon you unless you countersign the change and return to me a copy of this Release with the changes signed by you. This Release shall be governed and construed under the laws of California. Should any part of this Release be declared void, the remainder shall remain in full force and effect and at all times this Release shall be construed so as to carry out its intent.

Very truly yours,

_____   _____
Date   Signature

_____   _____
Telephone Number   Name (print)

                                     _____
                                     Address

                                     _____

ACKNOWLEDGED:

_____
Edwards Skerbelis Entertainment

_____
Name (print)

Option Agreement or Deal Memo

DISCLAIMER: DO NOT USE this option agreement "as is." It is meant only as an example, as the dollar figures may not be industry standard. Please consult an attorney or an agent whenever optioning a project.

DATE
NAME
ADDRESS
ADDRESS

Dear _____:

The following shall confirm the agreement between _____ (the "Writer") and Edwards Skerbelis Entertainment (the "Producers") with regard to the acquisition of an option to acquire all motion picture, television, allied and ancillary rights (the "Rights") to your screenplay (the "Property") currently titled _____.

1. <u>Option</u>: In consideration of the sum of one dollar ($1.00) and other good and valuable consideration, the receipt of which is hereby acknowledged, Writer hereby grants to Producers the exclusive, irrevocable option for a period of one (1) year upon execution of this Agreement to acquire the Rights.

2. <u>Option Extension</u>: Writer hereby grants to Producers the right to extend the option for an additional six months (6) commencing prior to the expiration of the initial option by written notice to Writer and payment of the sum of one hundred dollars ($100.00) which shall be applicable toward the Purchase Price. Writer hereby grants to Producers the right to extend the option a second time for an additional six months (6) commencing immediately upon the expiration of the first extension option by written notice to Writer and payment of the sum of Two Hundred and Fifty Dollars ($250.00) which shall be applicable toward the Purchase Price.

3. <u>Option Exercise</u>: Producers may exercise the option to acquire the Rights at any time during the option period or extended option period, if applicable, by written notice to Writer and payment of the sums set forth in paragraph 4 below.

4. <u>Purchase Price</u>: Upon exercise of the option, we shall pay Writer the following:

_____
(Name of Project/Writer's name)
as of _____Date
Page 2 of 5

a. If the project is intended as a theatrical motion picture, the Purchase Price shall be no less than Writers Guild of America scale plus ten percent (10%).

b. Writer may also be entitled to the following applicable bonus:

   i. If the budget is below Ten Million Dollars ($10,000,000.00) but greater than Three Million Dollars ($3,000,000.00) and Writer receives sole screenplay credit, Writer will receive an additional bonus of Fifty Thousand Dollars ($50,000.00). If the Writer shares screenplay credit with another writer, then Writer will receive an additional bonus of Twenty Five Thousand Dollars ($25,000.00); or

   ii. If the budget is below Twenty Million Dollars ($20,000,000.00) but more than Ten Million Dollars ($10,000,000.00) and Writer receives sole screenplay credit, Writer will receive an additional bonus of One Hundred Thousand Dollars ($100,000.00). If the Writer shares screenplay credit with another writer, then Writer will receive an additional bonus of Fifty Thousand Dollars ($50,000.00); or

   iii. If the budget is above Twenty Million Dollars ($20,000,000.00) and Writer receives sole screenplay credit there will be a bonus of One Hundred and Fifty Thousand Dollars ($150,000.00). If the Writer shares screenplay credit with another writer, Writer will receive a bonus of Fifty Thousand Dollars ($50,000.00).

c. If the initial Property is intended for pay cable such as HBO, Showtime, etc., and the final direct cost budget is Five Million Dollars ($5,000,000.00) or more, the Purchase Price shall be Seventy Five Thousand Dollars ($75,000.00). If the final direct cost budget is less than Five Million Dollars ($5,000,000.00), the Purchase Price shall be WGA scale plus Ten percent (10%).

d. If the initial project is intended for broadcast networks such as ABC, NBC, CBS, or Fox, the Purchase Price shall be WGA scale plus Ten percent (10%).

e. If the initial project is intended for basic cable, i.e., Lifetime, USA Network, UPN, SciFi Channel, etc., the Purchase Price shall be WGA scale plus Ten percent (10%).

f. Writer's services will be engaged to write at least one (1) rewrite and one (1) polish, with compensation at the applicable WGA minimum plus ten percent (10%) which shall be applicable against the Purchase Price per the WGA rules and regulations for such services.

_____
(Name of Project/Writer's name)
as of _____Date
Page 3 of 5

5. <u>Net Profits</u>: In addition to the Purchase Price and provided Writer receives sole screenplay credit on the motion picture ("Picture") produced hereunder, Writer shall be entitled to receive a sum equal to Five percent (5%) of One Hundred percent (100%) of the Net Profits of the Picture. If Writer receives shared screenplay credit Writer shall be entitled to Two and One-Half percent (2 1/2%) of One Hundred percent (100%) of the Net Profits of the Picture. Net profits shall be defined as deficit financiers standard definition of Net Profits at the time, exclusive of cross collateralization and overbudget penalties.

6. <u>Sequels/Remakes</u>: For each Sequel or Remake of the Picture Writer shall receive the following:

a. Sequels: Fifty percent (50%) of the Purchase Price plus bonus if applicable and Net Profits unless the Sequel is for a different media (as defined in paragraphs 6 (c) below).

b. Remakes: Thirty-Three and One Third percent (33 1/3%) of the Purchase Price plus bonus if applicable and Net Profits unless the Remake is for a different media (as defined in paragraphs 6 (c) below).

c. If the Sequel or Remake is for a different media (different media to be defined but not limited to video games, CD-Roms, CD-I's, on-line services, interactive television, interactive media or any other technology now in existence or hereafter devised), then the payment for such Sequels or Remakes shall be negotiated in good faith for that applicable media in keeping within the industry standards for such media.

7. <u>Television Series</u>: If a television series is produced based on the Property the purchase price will be in accordance with WGA minimums and good faith negotiations and Writer shall receive a royalty for each new episode produced payable on completion of production of each episode depending on the length as follows:

      30 minute $1,551.00
      60 minute $2,947.00
      90 minute or longer $3,878.00

Plus 100% of that amount spread over the first five (5) reruns.

8. <u>Additional Mini-Series and MOWS</u>:

a. <u>MOW</u>: If the initial picture is produced as a theatrical and then remade as a movie-of-the-week, Writer shall receive Twenty Thousand Dollars ($20,000.00) for the first two hours and Five Thousand Dollars ($5,000.00) for each additional hour thereafter, payable within Ten (10) days of the initial broadcast of such movie-of-the-week.

(Name of Project/Writer's name)
as of _____Date
Page 4 of 5

b. <u>Mini-Series</u>: If the initial picture is produced as a theatrical and then remade as a mini-series for television, Writer shall receive Thirty Thousand Dollars ($30,000.00) for the first two hours and Ten Thousand Dollars ($10,000.00) for each additional hour thereafter up to a maximum of Eighty Thousand Dollars ($80,000.00) for the entire mini-series, payable within Ten (10) days of the initial broadcast of such mini-series.

c. If the initial movie for television is released as a theatrical motion picture in the United States prior to its television broadcast, Writer shall receive One Hundred percent (100%) of the movie of the week purchase price outlined in Paragraph 4 c, d, and e above.

d. If the initial movie for television is released in the foreign market as a theatrical movie prior to its United States television broadcast, Writer shall receive Fifty percent (50%) of the movie of the week purchase priced outlined in Paragraph 4 c, d, and e above.

e. If the picture is released theatrically after the U.S. television broadcast, Writer shall receive Fifty percent (50%) of the movie of the week purchase price outlined in Paragraph 4 c, d and e above.

9. <u>Payment</u>: Writer will be paid in a timely manner per WGA provisions.

10. <u>Setup Bonus</u>:

a. Upon setup of the Picture as a feature film at a major studio, Writer shall receive a bonus of Seven Thousand Five Hundred Dollars ($7,500.00) which will be applicable towards the Purchase Price.

b. Upon setup of the Picture as a feature film at a non-major studio, Writer shall receive a bonus of Five Thousand Dollars ($5,000.00) which will be applicable towards the Purchase Price.

c. Upon the setup of the Picture as a television or cable film, Writer shall receive a bonus of Two Thousand Five Hundred Dollars ($2,500.00) which will be applicable towards the Purchase Price.

(Name of Project/Writer's name)
as of _____Date
Page 5 of 5

11. <u>Representation and Warranties</u>: The Writer warrants and represents that: (a) the Property is original with Writer; (b) neither the Property nor any element thereof nor the exploitation thereof does or will in any way infringe upon or violate any copyright, or the best of Writer's knowledge violate the right of privacy or publicity, common law rights, or any other rights, or constitute a libel or slander against any person, firm or corporation whomsoever; (c) Writer owns all right, title and interest in and to the Property free and clear of any liens, encumbrances and other third party interests of any kind, and free of any claims or litigation, whether pending or threatened; (d) Writer has the full right and power to make and perform this Agreement without the consent of any third party; (e) the Property has not previously been exploited in any dramatic or audiovisual media, whether as a motion picture, television production, play or otherwise, and no rights have been granted to any third parties to do so; and (f) Writer is the author and owner of the Property, and entitled to all copyrights therein forever, with the right to make such changes therein and uses thereof as Writer may determine as author.

Writer hereby indemnifies Producers against any and all claims, costs, losses, damages, or expenses (including reasonable attorneys fees and costs) asserted against and/or incurred by reason of any actual or alleged breach of the foregoing representations and warranties.

12. <u>Other Terms and Conditions</u>: Other terms and conditions including without limitation warranties and indemnities, waiver of so-called "droit-morale" and the like shall be in accordance with standard terms applicable to deals of this nature within the entertainment industry. A more formal agreement between the parties may be entered into to incorporate such provisions as well as the terms set forth in this letter agreement. Until such formal agreement is entered into, if ever, this letter agreement shall constitute a binding agreement between the parties.

Very truly yours,

_____
(Individual's Name)
(Production Company Name)

AGREED TO AND ACCEPTED:

_____
Date

_____
Writer

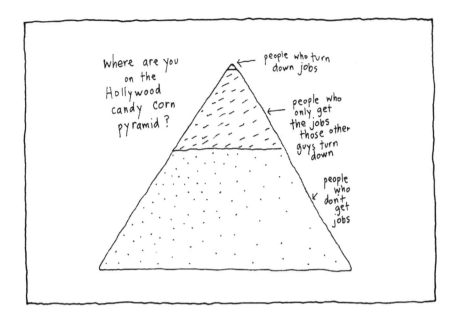

where are you
on the
Hollywood
candy corn
pyramid?

people who turn
down jobs

people who
only get
the jobs
those other
guys turn
down

people
who
don't
get
jobs

7

"The Chicken or the Egg"

working for a producer, director, or an actor vs. a studio

By now you know there are many possibilities in the world of development and many types of jobs available. Whether you work for a studio or a production company, you have many options. While the basics for developing movies remains the same, the needs of the studio or production company may differ.

WORKING FOR A TALENT-DRIVEN COMPANY

More and more studios are making deals with talent-driven production companies. Big stars and successful directors often end up with term deals at the studio where their last movie was made. With those deals usually comes a staff consisting of a development executive and an assistant, though some talent have producing partners and some are so wildly successful they have a larger staff with numerous development execs; some even have their own business affairs departments.

Working for a producer differs from working for talent, such as a director who has a production company, in that the creative executive is involved with finding material that the director might actually want to direct rather than just produce. This would also apply for an actor's production company. Most studio deals with directors or actors allow for some possibility that the talent will be involved solely as a producer but the studio is always hopeful that talent will actually direct or star in the movie. The talent is the engine that drives the projects forward. Should the finished script meet the director or actor's approval, he or she might decide to star in or direct the film their own production company is developing, but they are not formally committed to the project other than producing it. Sometimes talent will use their clout to accelerate a production slate of movies for their production company to produce by dangling their own involvement as more than just a producer on the project. A lot of times, this is the way they will get projects into development with a studio while still not committing to actually directing or starring in the movie. The studio wants to accommodate their star artists and in so doing will put many of their most marketable projects into the pipeline in order to keep them happy.

By having a successful production company with some power, an actor or director can do passion projects along with studio fare. This can allow them to work with material that is edgy and not normally found on a studio slate. It also gives them a chance to expand and challenge themselves. Sometimes talent is required to star in or direct a negotiated number of movies for a particular studio within a specific time frame. A studio may develop a project with the talent's production company knowing that it may be one of the "committed" projects outlined in the talent's two-picture deal, for example.

As an executive working for a company run by talent, there is enormous opportunity to use celebrity name value to get in many doors and meet as many people as possible. Whether using the muscle of the company to get agents to submit their more high-profile material or pitching their company's projects to studios and other production companies, an executive can be very visible and aggressively promote his company's agenda. That being said it is still important for the executive to be in tune with what type of material the talent gravitates towards as well as maintain the status quo in the industry. Certain directors and actors are known for specific genres—while they may want to expand into other arenas, the studio expects them to maintain their box office clout with films similar to those that have been successful for them in the past. The development executive must be aware of all these issues, specifically focusing on his company's development needs.

WORKING FOR A PRODUCER

A producer, on the other hand, might have to attach talent to a script in order to make it more attractive to a studio. As already discussed, this is called packaging. Agents have been known to package material and sometimes they will help a producer secure talent. Of course, they will commission the producer for this service. Producers, most likely, will have a wider range of material and are not limited to doing the same genre pictures over and over (unless, of course, that's what the producer wants to do).

Working for a producer can provide a development executive with a more hands-on situation. If the producer is one who really finds the material, develops it, sets it up, casts it, and sees it through production and delivery, the development executive can be the right-hand person to that producer. This gives the executive the opportunity to move up the ladder toward being a producer himself, gaining the experience needed by working for a true producer.

Some producers are known for certain types of material but, most likely, there will be a much wider variety of genres for a development executive to sink their teeth into, as well as seeking an unlimited range of new material. It is important to gauge what the producer's taste actually is and find stories that will get them excited, stories they can feel passionate about. Feature films take so long to get made, that it is important to find and work on material that everyone loves because you will be working on it for a very long time and must not tire of it. Producers who have term deals at studios will have more leverage getting top spec scripts from top agents. As a development executive working for one of these companies, you need to be networking, tracking, and developing agent relationships to make sure you get that material. A top producer will yell and scream at their development exec if, come Monday, a script is set up at their home studio and their company didn't even receive it. It is up to the development executive to stay on top of all new material, find new talent, seek out books not on the market yet, and bring in material that the studio will buy. It is no good for an executive to keep submitting to his studio and getting passes. It is important to know the difference between good material and mediocrity. Granted, we have all seen movies and wondered how they were ever sold to begin with, but sometimes it was a better screenplay than it was a movie. However, it is important to know the studio executives and familiarize yourself with what sort of projects will appeal to a particular executive.

Working for a producer offers a great opportunity to not only learn the trade of producing, but also to recognize material that services the taste of the company and the studio it is supplying.

WORKING FOR A STUDIO VS. A PRODUCTION COMPANY

Studio creative executives have a stronger need to fill the pipeline with product and rely on their term deal production companies as well as outside "indie" companies to furnish them with suitable material. We reiterate that as a studio executive, you are the buyer...though you must convince your creative team to buy the material or screenplay. It is your responsibility to oversee and move a project towards a greenlight. You must be able to collaborate with the writer and producers involved, give notes that will help the project, and get the project in shape so that the head of production will give it the blessing it needs to go to production. As powerful as the position of studio creative executive might seem to be, it is a lot of work to oversee projects in various stages of development and production, network with agents, managers, producers, and production company executives, to try and move things forward.

Working for a production company, you are both buyer and seller. The production company executive needs to find material and create a slate of movies to produce, but usually with limited funds. Executives at production companies need to be able to set material up at studios or indie finance companies and then oversee the development and eventual production of the script. They must be able to identify strong *marketable* material and also be able to convince the writer or writer's representation to allow the executive the opportunity to run with it. Sometimes, there may be funds to do a small option, other times, the executive will have a limited leash (along with other production companies) to try to set up the project at a studio. A successful executive working for a producer at a production company must know the marketplace. While their boss will focus on the nitty gritty of producing the movie, the development executive can be influential in introducing new talent to their bosses, or bringing in material that is innovative and fresh, and thereby make a name for themselves by having a successful record for setting up studio movies.

NEW PRODUCERS

Working as a development executive is a natural opening for becoming a producer. The relationships with talent, the experience developing new material, working with writers, putting projects together, setting them up, and getting them made is a good segue into becoming an independent producer. A number of studio development executives, upon expiration of their contracts, are given producer term deals to kick-start their producing careers.

New producers, who have been developing material on their own but do not have the exposure or experience to be recognized by a major studio, should consider partnering with a producer who does have that experience. Hollywood is always hungry for new and fresh material. If it's good, a new producer can interest a more seasoned producer fairly easily. What this often does, however, is relegate the new producer to the sidelines. The more experienced producer will run the show while the new producer may be ignored. This very common occurrence makes it important that, as a new producer, you insist *contractually* to be involved with the project and earn your producer or executive producer credit.

CONCLUSION

There are so many stories told by development executives and producers about the long and arduous journey of developing a screenplay into a movie. Sometimes these stories require Kleenex. Most times, they're "also-rans"—meaning the movie got made but it didn't cause any great waves of glory. The fact that anything ever gets made in this town should be celebrated, really.

There is great power working for a studio. But with that power comes limitation. It's like having an exclusive deal. The executive gets one shot to sell his colleagues on a project he feels passionate about and, if they pass and he can't muster any support from the head of production, it's over for that project at that studio. One studio executive confided to us, "Working for a studio has the greatest perks. You never have to pay for anything. My meals are paid for...I never have to pay for a movie or theatre tickets, video rentals, and I even get a car allowance. All my entertainment is paid for, not to mention all the invitations to premieres and awards ceremonies. It's the greatest job in the world *as long as you're successful at it.*" This is a business of perks. But while the glitter of success may be appealing, actually reaching that goal is a long and demanding process.

Working for a production company, whether it's talent driven or run by a bona fide producer, can be limitless. If the company is in a first look deal, they have other shots to set up material at competing studios, not to mention the possibility of setting the movie up for television. There is a greater opportunity for advancement by starting out working for a production company and easier access to a production company job vs. a studio position. No matter how difficult it is to buy or sell a project, when it gets made, the reward is greater than the painful journey it may have required. There is great satisfaction in seeing an idea become a screenplay and then become a movie.

However, development jobs can be like revolving doors. People are always going out one door and opening another; moving from one company to another or from a studio or network and back again to a production company or independent producing deal. To keep working as a development executive, the person must not only be good at what he or she does, but also know how to maneuver the politics of getting along with many high-spirited, aggressive, and artistic people. A successful executive must be able to fight for what they believe in yet not step on any powerful toes. Good taste is not always a prerequisite for success in this business, but it does help to know good material, the marketability and commercial prospects of that material, and how to sell it. This is a necessary attribute regardless of whether you work for a studio or a production company.

We sometimes take for granted the kind of lifestyle we are privileged to live by working in the entertainment industry. There is nothing else like it on earth but it's not all glamour and it certainly doesn't come easily. In order to succeed, the focus must truly be on finding the projects, and then pushing them relentlessly without giving up. It's having drive and ambition. This is an industry where most "overnight successes" have been working... for fifteen years.

8

"It All Began With the Written Word..."

the writer

The screenwriter is the backbone of the industry. Sometimes they are cast aside too soon, replaced by others, used and abused...but without them, there would be no movies. Writers are the ones who start out with a blank piece of paper and fill that page with story. From that one blank piece of paper is born a screenplay. If it ain't on the page, it ain't on the stage. Directors might rewrite them, actors may challenge the dialogue, a producer may offer strong suggestions or changes to the material, but through it all, it always starts with the writer. This truly collaborative medium kick starts with the writer's words, which are then handed over to a producer and/or director to fully realize on the silver screen.

With over 40,000 screenplays registered at the Writers Guild of America every year, and 5,000 scripts submitted to each studio, not to mention the production company submissions, the question comes up—how do writers get their scripts noticed out of the myriad of stories that pass through an executive's hands on a weekly basis? And, once the executive recognizes a good screenplay and gets it set up at a studio or a production company, how does the executive work with the writer to make the necessary changes in order to get the studio to give it a greenlight? In turn, how does the writer work with the producer and studio executive?

Writers usually believe their material is ready to be shot. However, they are not always the best judges when it comes to their own stories. They're just too close to the work. Enter a producer and/or development executive who helps mold and shape the script into a "shootable" movie. It's not always easy and it might even take more than one writer (and many creative executions) to get it in front of the camera.

A lot of times, writers can be defensive when given notes, and either shoot themselves in the foot by ignoring the development notes or get bogged down arguing over minor details that often don't even affect the outcome of their story. In return, the movie doesn't get made. Screenwriters can be *too* accommodating as well—when the writer follows the notes explicitly without standing up for specific points that work best for the story, thereby caving into others' opinions and going against the writers own inclinations and creativity...and still the movie doesn't get made! It's a delicate balance. So, in giving and receiving notes, how *do* the writer, producer, and executive achieve a delicate balance of being able to recognize what is:

- Good for the studio or production company.
- Good for the screenplay.
- Good for getting the movie produced.
- Good for the writer's career.
- Good for the producer's and/or executive's career.

Writers tend to forget that the studio or indie finance company is ultimately footing the bill and if the buyers can't get what they want, why should they pay for it? Again, this is not to say that a writer should just be "a lamb trotting along to the slaughter," but rather that screenwriters need to know when to fight what battle, and when to try and make the script work to satisfy the powers that be (who sign the checks).

THE WRITER—RECEIVING DEVELOPMENT NOTES

No one wants to rewrite their work. It can be long, tedious, and laborious. But as we've stated over and over, the film business is a collaborative effort and writers must realize that in order to climb up the ladder of success in this business, they must be willing and able to recognize that notes, rewrites, polishes, and being rewritten by someone else, are all part of this collective process. If a writer does not want to take notes or make changes; if he simply does not want to rewrite his material, then he should be a playwright. The film business is not for him. The Dramatists Guild (which governs writers in the theatre) is very clear that no one can change a word, a line, or even a punctuation mark without the writer's permission. In contrast, when it comes to the medium of film, it is always about the rewrite and a writer has to be resigned to that fact or change professions.

So, how should a writer approach taking notes from executives and producers? One of the key components is "listening" and having an open mind. Be flexible. As the writer, you don't have to agree or disagree to anything up front. Take it all in, then if some things stand out as a problem, you can bring it up with an eye toward brainstorming for solutions. Sometimes a studio exec has no time for this and the writer should be able to recognize this and take up his or her concerns with the producer or the production company executive. Sometimes out of that brainstorming comes an even better idea, so it's important, if at all possible, to engage in this kind of scenario in order to dig deeper into the script to bring out more story possibilities. The writer should not over-analyze the notes, especially in a meeting. We've been with writers who have to discuss every note and the meeting lasted for hours when it should have only lasted maybe one—not a good thing to do! No one has the time and everyone expects the writer to just "get it."

If the writer receives a note they strongly disagree with, or maybe even sounds ludicrous, it is important to understand where that note is coming from—the rationale behind it and why it is necessary to change it. Of course, "bad" notes are always difficult to handle...no one wants to hear negativity. So, how do you refuse the note without insulting the source? The best way is to engage that person in a conversation in order to get to the core of the note and, hopefully, the note will then start to make sense. Sometimes it's just a "bad" note. However, more times than not, through discussion, notes become clearer to all involved. Sometimes notes can be very generic and it's difficult for a writer to grasp the specifics.

Be aware that if the studio and writer come to an impasse, it would behoove the writer, as well as the producer, to be flexible. You can risk standing your ground but remember: the studio is footing the bill and the writer can be replaced. However, that being said, if there is a disagreement, a good backup argument will most certainly go a long way and convince a good executive to fight for the original vision of the project. Countless times, if the writer explains and backs up his decisions or his angle on the story with a strong argument, an executive will see clearly the writer's intention and the writer will understand what is not clear in his story.

No one should get mad if a writer requires more details. A producer also can be very helpful in conveying the meaning and particulars of any given note. But all parties should strive to be as unambiguous as possible, again to make sure that all are on the same page and the screenplay is what everyone expects it to be. Communication is a key ingredient in the development process.

Sometimes, the writer may latch onto a note and run with it and all its potential, spouting off ideas and ways to execute the note, and this may energize the room. It is important to engage the executive and producers in developing your ideas. That is, if they are brainstorming and getting excited about the new ideas, they will become more emotionally invested in the project and encourage you to realize those ideas.

So, the writer gets his first set of notes and goes home to figure out how to execute them. After much thought, and maybe even putting something on paper, the writer might want to have another meeting with either the producer or studio exec (or both) in order to make sure the rewrite is going in the right direction. If a writer gets stumped, he should think of the production company as being a conduit to help him over the humps. The producer or development executive can brainstorm, make suggestions, and offer overall support and encouragement to the writer. Depending on the relationship with the studio executive, a writer should always go through the producer on the project first (if there is one) unless the producer suggests talking to the studio executive as well.

Once the studio, producer, and writer have signed off on the changes to be made, the writer sits at his computer, pounding out the revisions, and executing them the best way he can. Usually, the writer has a deadline of four to eight weeks to deliver the first rewrite.

So, let's assume the writer has completed his rewrite. He will then hand it into the producer and there might be a few tweaks made to the material before sending it over to the studio. Once everyone feels it's ready, it is then given to the studio and is considered an official *delivery*.

THE STUDIO'S RESPONSE

The contractual "step" the writer is on will affect the quickness of the studio's response to the producer and the writer. For example, if it is a *committed* or *guaranteed step* (meaning the writer still owes another draft per the negotiated agreement) then the studio could take up to four weeks to read the script, called a *reading period,* and compile notes. Most times, it's sooner. There will most likely be another *notes* meeting with the writer and producer, though sometimes the exec may just give the notes to the producer to convey to the writer.

If the next writing step is *optional*, meaning there are no other committed steps to the deal, and if the studio elects to continue with that writer, they will have to negotiate another fee or exercise the optional step from the original agreement. Then, the exec may place the just-delivered screenplay on the weekend read. Come Monday morning's staff meeting, a decision will be made whether to continue with this writer or cut this writer loose and hire a new one, thus making it an open writing assignment. However, if there are any doubts about the project itself, it may also be placed in turnaround—which generally means the project is dead at that studio.

The writer, if replaced, should not beat himself up. It is standard operating procedure for a studio to feel that the writer has taken it as far as he or she can and a new writer will bring fresh ideas to the piece and move it along towards the greenlight. Sometimes, as the writer, you may feel as though you've done all you can with the material and you may not want to do any more rewrites. Being rewritten is like giving your baby up for adoption; you're never sure if you're going to see it again.

It is very rare and most improbable that a studio will buy a script and shoot it "as is." There can be multiple drafts of the screenplay and sometimes a writer is rewritten several times by other writers. This should not discourage you, though it is sometimes hard to handle being replaced. Usually, if the studio brings on other writers, it's because they want to make the movie work, and the extra money invested in rewrites will make the project more likely to be completed, as the studio always wants to recoup its investment. Of course, there are always exceptions to the rule.

If there is more than one writer on a project and there is a dispute as to each writer's contribution, it is up to the Writers Guild of America's arbitration committee to decide on who receives credit for the screenplay and story. It is not the studio. It is not the producer. It is not the writer. It is a committee made up of WGA peers who review the different drafts without knowing who actually wrote which version (the writers' names are removed from the title pages). They decide whether or not an original screenplay has been changed more than 50 percent by subsequent writers other than the original writer(s). That would require an awful lot of changes to the material. It would mean that the plot, characters, and dialogue would have to have a complete overhaul for any additional writers to receive writing credit alongside the original writer. The Guild is asked more than one hundred and fifty times a year in feature films and more than three hundred times a year in television to resolve issues between writers over their credits. This is the way the Guild protects writers from personal clashes and also ensures the official writer's credit upon which the talent depends.

WORKING FOR A WRITER'S COMPANY

Most writers do not have actual production companies. If a writer does have a production company, there is usually a development executive on board as well. Some writers oversee other writers, some want to direct, and others want to produce other people's material. Working for a writer requires different strengths. Giving notes to a boss on the boss' own screenplays can be a very sensitive process. However, most likely, the executive will be out scouting for material just like any other development executive, but more with an eye for the writer to produce.

Some writers help out other writers. They will guarantee the studio a good script by overseeing a younger, up-and-coming writer. They do this because they may love the story, believe in the talent, and want to get involved as a producer. Lending their name to the project gives it more credibility and is more of an insurance policy for the studio.

Some writers will have an assistant who handles more than just administrative responsibilities. The assistant may also do research on projects, take dictation, and ready a screenplay in proper format, to name a few of the duties. Working for a writer can be good training and a stepping-stone for becoming a writer or a development executive.

CONCLUSION

Producers, directors, actors, and studios need writers. It all begins with the written word. However, writers need studios, producers, directors, and actors to bring about the complete realization of their stories. They need development executives to find their material, to bring it to the attention of the powers that be, and also to recommend them for open writing assignments. It's not enough to just have a good script; you need a good team to help bring it to the silver screen. And that is the ultimate goal for everyone.

9

"The Times They Are 'A Changin'"
networking, tracking, and the internet

Today's changing technology has only served to help the development process. Some of the strongest development executives know how to track material, network with colleagues, and cultivate new relationships. Information is key and with the advent of the Internet, it is easier than ever before for executives, writers, and producers to gain access to film data, keep up with filmmakers around the world, share information, and keep tabs on the latest happenings in the film industry. However, developing personal relationships with others is still the most important facet of getting ahead in the film business. It is through these relationships that information is shared and careers are made. So, how do you meet those people? Who are they? Where are they?

NETWORKING

There are many organizations an up-and-coming producer, writer, or development exec can join to help navigate the waters of the industry. The IFP, Women in Film (WIF), monthly networking breakfasts, film festivals, and screenings are all great ways to meet people who have the same goals. Classes at many of the universities and junior colleges as well as private workshops and seminars are other ways of meeting new people. It is important to start developing your own Rolodex by collecting business cards and keeping up with those contacts. Some industrious people will start their own networking groups, meeting once a week or once a month, and discuss the latest goings-on or share information about new writers or filmmakers. Others have a regular poker or basketball game (deals have been made shooting hoops!). Breakfast, lunch, dinner, drinks, and even coffee meetings are terrific ways to begin business relationships and create friendships. There isn't a day that goes by in the movie industry when a producer doesn't hook up with another industry person or development executive and after first asking, "How are you?" following it up with, "What are *you* looking for?" And if more than two people get together and talk about someone else that they just met with, you can bet those other people will ask, "What are *they* looking for?" With time, you will find the more you network, the more people you will know, and the more your clique will expand—thus creating opportunities for jobs, script sales, and guidance along the way. If you're working as an assistant, you talk to many people through the course of the day. A good suggestion would be is to invite one of them, or their assistants, out for coffee or drinks and pick their brains about a specific area of interest.

THE INTERNET AND E-MAIL

With e-mail, it's much easier to keep in contact with people. Some groups only correspond via e-mail and have chat rooms to converse about the latest movies. Because of e-mail, you can keep in contact with people from other cities around the world. It's a fast, inexpensive, and easy way to communicate without taking up a lot of time. Some executives, producers, agents, and managers prefer e-mail to the phone because it's quick and can be done at their leisure and not take up valuable business time.

The Internet also offers databases useful in creating lists of actors, writers, and directors. There are Web sites that track movies in production and development, as well as sites offering screenplays for downloading, contact information, and box office information. Additionally, you can access headlines and stories from *The Hollywood Reporter* and *Daily Variety* Web sites. There is a comprehensive list of various, helpful Internet Web sites found in Chapter 13 titled "Resources."

TRACKING BOARDS

One of the most helpful late 20th Century creations for development executives was the invention of the "Tracking Board." Originally started by Roy Lee, now a successful producer (*The Ring*, 2002 and *The Ring Two*, 2005), tracking boards are simply Web sites in which production company executives list scripts that agents and/or managers are going out with to the town. Each executive has to be a member of the tracking board and usually is invited to be so or sometimes they start their own tracking group and hand-pick the members who belong.

Once the script is listed on the tracking board by one of the members, other production company executives who belong to that board and have not received a phone call from the writer's representative, respond by calling the agent or manager wanting to get a copy of the script. This creates "heat" for the project by alerting those executives who may not have been on the agent's or manager's list for initial submissions. In turn, they try to get the material submitted to their company. It's also a way for members of the tracking board to share information quickly. Sometimes a development exec may add comments to the board (for example, if there are any elements [talent] attached, if it's going into a studio, or even if they liked the script or not). While tracking boards still exist today, most have morphed into member-only discussion groups and email rather than a website dedicated for members to log into as illustrated in this chapter.

Agents have a love/hate relationship with tracking boards. They love the heat they can create and hate it if a negative comment prevents the

Tracking Board Sample

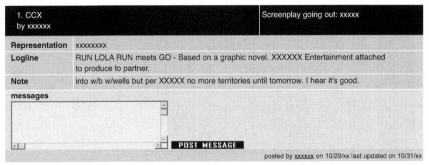

script from moving forward. Sometimes agents will make a request that the development executive not put a project on a tracking board. But, it is a small town and it's amazing how many people know about something they're not supposed to know about. All in all, the tracking board is self-run, and a way for executives to give and receive information about scripts going out to the town.

CONCLUSION

Today's world offers so much information and technology without the expense and time it used to take to acquire this data. With all the machinery, it still comes down to human contact, relationships, and building those relationships. From the moment you make your first phone call, attend your first class, or have your first networking meeting, the associations forged from those experiences can last your whole career. You grow up together, you help each other, and you relish in each other's success (hopefully). The more you meet and greet, the bigger your Rolodex.

Socializing is a prerequisite for a beginning executive, producer, writer, agent, or assistant hoping to get ahead. We can't stress enough how important it is to network in this business, to know people, to give and take in business relationships, and not be afraid to make that first phone call. The nervous sweat on your forehead will be worth the excruciating pain of punching that number. You'd be surprised; most people are fairly accessible and those who aren't at first, will most likely become accessible in time. Above all, it is about having something worthwhile to contribute—whether it's information, a project, or a helping hand.

With computers, the Internet, and affordable software, life as a development executive, producer, director, writer, agent, or manager has become more and more obtainable. Prices are decreasing, making it affordable for anyone of any stature to own the basics that can help get them started. For five thousand dollars, you can have your own production and editing studio in your house. Most tracking boards are free. Research on the Internet is mostly free or more reasonably priced from some of the top industry-standard Internet services. Information is everywhere and it's there for the taking. It is up to you to grab hold and run with it.

EXERCISE

Find and attend a film networking function. Check out Chapter 13—"Resources" for hints.

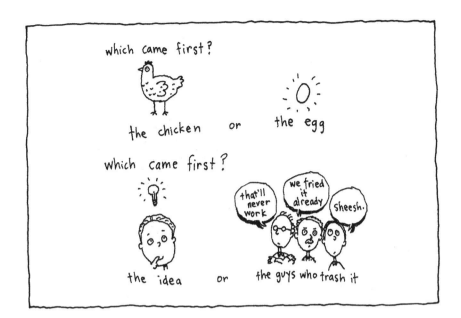

10

"If There Are Only Seven Plotlines, How Come I Have So Many Stories?"
finding ideas

Ideas can come from many places. While not all of them are translatable to film, some of the best films come from ideas based upon other source material. It is not just enough to find screenplays from writers. Producers, development executives, and studios must be able to create ideas from within as well. They must seek out material that is not always from normal suppliers such as agents. They must dig for potential stories via unusual sources. There are many ways to find material and numerous possibilities in cultivating ideas. The sky is the limit.

What is a good idea, anyway? Can it be defined? How do you recognize one? We get asked these questions all the time and they're difficult to answer. A good idea is a story or a concept that you feel passionate about that can be translated cinematically to the movie screen. A good idea is oftentimes subjective but it's usually something that other people respond to (besides yourself). Something that is accessible to an audience and yet can be a commercial success; that can possibly enlighten the public and entertain them, as well as attract A-list talent. A good idea may have a strong hook to it or may offer a different perspective on subject matter already seen in previous movies. A good idea for a movie is a movie you, yourself, want to go see and are willing to pay the ten spot to see it.

Being aware that you can find great stories in everyday life is essential to anyone who wants to make good movies. Ideas can come from newspapers, magazines, and the Internet. Sometimes, you can find ideas just by people watching. The important thing to remember is that ideas are everywhere and as a development executive, writer, producer, or director, you must be aware of what's going on around you at all times. In everything, there is potential for a story and it can sometimes come from the most surprising places. Where do ideas come from? Where do you start looking for them? Here are just a few thoughts on where to begin:

- Brainstorming sessions to come up with ideas and potential concepts
- Searching through magazines and newspapers for articles
- Surfing the Internet for potential stories
- Books—both fiction and non-fiction
- Short Stories
- True Life Stories
- Obituaries (don't laugh—there can be some great stories in those obits)
- Comic Books
- Graphic Novels
- Historical events
- Plays
- Foreign language films remade into English language films
- Remakes and Redos
- Video Games

This is just a jumping off point for finding material. There are so many more places to dig for ideas than what we've mentioned above. However, using these may start you in the right direction.

IDENTIFYING STORIES

Brainstorming

Many production companies and some studios will have brainstorming meetings. Executives and producers will toss around concepts with each other for potential motion pictures and, in turn, stories may develop. There may be arenas that a company or producer wants to explore, i.e., surfing, Wall Street, horseracing. This arena could become the core of an idea and, from that, writers may be interviewed to come up with an original take on that central thought which then could be pitched to a studio.

Newspapers and Magazines

One of the first places to look for ideas is in newspapers and magazines. Not only can you find true-life stories, but there also might be social references from which a story can be built. It might be an article about a tree that needs to be moved and causes an uproar in the community, a whistle-blower's story like Erin Brockovich, a human rights issue, or it even can be a story created from an advertising line from a magazine ad. It might be a story that is dramatic or even comical. Just because it's in a newspaper doesn't mean it can't be entertaining.

Some of the best articles from newspapers have been found in small town presses. While it's true that the *New York Times* and other big national newspapers have great stories, an up-and-coming producer or writer might have better luck acquiring the rights to an article from a small town paper. With the Internet, it is now possible to surf the web for these newspapers and find a whole myriad of potential stories. Touchstone's *Calendar Girls* (2003) was based upon articles found in a newspaper about middle-aged women who bared their breasts for a calendar in Northern England in order to raise money for the local hospital.

While newspapers offer the world as it's happening on a daily basis with a purely journalistic approach, magazines, oftentimes, comment on what's already happened or spotlight human interest stories. For example, there was an article in a major publication about a teacher whose students took out an ad in the personals—not only did they get her a date, she married the guy nine months later. This article, discovered by Rona, was seen as a romantic comedy and put into development at a major studio. The article was barely one page but it caught her eye and the next thing you know, it's a deal at a studio. Sometimes an article might just have a terrific headline—and that's enough to develop a movie from it. "Cop Gives Waitress $2 Million Tip!" became *It Could Happen To You* (1994) starring Nicholas Cage and Bridget Fonda.

Another example is when the article is actually about something else but something within the piece has potential on its own to be a totally different story. For example, an article Monika found about spies being caught, leaving their wives to fend for themselves, may actually be a movie about the wives in the same vein as *The First Wives Club* (1996), only now we've spun it into *Spy Wives* which we are currently developing with producer, Cari-Esta Albert (*The Truth About Cats and Dogs*). It's about looking for the story within the story. It's about being aware of other possibilities and not just what's on the page.

But how do you know what makes a good movie from the articles you read everyday? First off, there has to be a concept that can be identified as visual storytelling. Next, there must be interesting characters to drive the story. And lastly, it must appeal to buyers as a television movie, studio feature, or independent film.

Television News
Watching the local or national news on cable or network television can often reveal stories that might make good movies. Usually these are human-interest stories, but work in much the same way as a newspaper or magazine article.

Surfing the Net
With the advent of the Internet, there are countless Web sites to peruse and unearth innumerable story possibilities. Every newspaper and magazine has a Web site highlighting the many stories in their own communities along with national/international news and human-interest articles. However, sometimes an idea for a story may not be in the news of the Net, but in other aspects of Web surfing, i.e., the personals and games. Again, it's about seeing beyond the obvious to come up with new, original, and fresh ideas that can be translated into film. One click can lead to many stories.

Books, Short Stories, and True-Life Stories
Books, short stories, and true-life stories have always been the backbone of the movie industry. "Ripped from the headlines" has been a staple in television movies going back at least to 1969 when the "movie of the week" first hit the scene. True-life stories exhibiting spirit and inspiration or shedding light on scandals and events can find a home in both television and the movie theatre.

Books and short stories have always been wonderful sources. Fiction or non-fiction, it doesn't matter as long as it's a good yarn. However, book rights are not always easy to obtain without a lot of money, especially if the book is a bestseller. In light of that, it might be best to focus on smaller press books, foreign books, as well as older books that have somehow been overlooked by the film community. Sometimes an author will respond to the passion of a writer or producer even if they are not household names. If the production company has a studio deal, they might, in conjunction with that studio, negotiate a respectable deal for the rights. Naturally, an author's agent or publishing house would prefer the latter. But it is not impossible to get an author to make a deal with a new producer who doesn't have tons of money, especially if the producer's "take" on the material coincides with the author's own. For example, John Irving granted rights for his bestseller *A Widow for One Year*, to a promising filmmaker, which became the movie *The Door in the Floor* (2004). It's about gaining their trust. The point is you must try and, if they refuse, so be it, but at least you tried to get the rights.

We had a student in one of our classes whose assignment was to find an article that could be made into a movie. Through some detective work, she contacted one of the people in the story to obtain the rights and managed to get him to agree to let her try and set it up. She then contacted a famous writer, sold him on the story, and got him involved. Whether or not this movie ever sees the light of day, it doesn't matter. She saw the potential and went after it. She was also proven right in her instincts because another proven professional saw what she saw in the story.

Fairy tales are also a good resource of material as are classic stories done in a contemporary setting. The films *Roxanne* (1987) and *The Truth About Cats and Dogs* (1996) were both a modern day retelling of *Cyrano de Bergerac* and some version of *Cinderella* appears almost every year.

Another possible source for material may come from bookstores located in small towns. They usually have a regional or local section of books by writers living in the area. Sometimes these books offer the history of the area and sometimes they tell a personal story. This is another great resource for finding fresh ideas while on vacation. The point is *you're always looking* for ideas.

Obituaries

Another great place to look for stories is in the obituaries. Normal, everyday people can still lead extraordinary lives. In obituaries, you can find quirky, surprising, and unusual characters whose lives could translate to the big screen. Sometimes it's who they are, other times it can be about what they've done for their community, or maybe something more personal pertaining to their own family. Obituaries should not be overlooked when it comes to finding new ideas.

Comic Books and Graphic Novels

Comic books have always made their way on to the screen. Unfortunately, most of them are owned by syndicates, which usually are subsidiaries of studios, thereby making it almost impossible for a newer producer or writer to option the work. However, if you are a producer with a studio deal and the studio has a backlog of material that they own which has never been made, it would behoove you to find that one comic book in their archives, come up with a fresh and original take, and convince the studio to put it into development.

Today, with computer generated images (CGI), comic books come to life in a more realistic manner than ever proving that anything can now be done on the screen as long as you have the money to pay for it.

One of the newer waves of material Hollywood is currently infatuated with is called the "graphic novel." This is a book of pictures that tells a story graphically. It's like a comic book but is considered its own genre. It is usually a long-form book rather than a comic book and is more similar to a novel than a short story. Originally, the term "graphic novel" was used by authors wanting to differentiate their work from the lighter fare intended for children. Much credit is given to Will Eisner for the development of this writing style. Eisner, a comic strip artist in the 40s, introduced what we now call the "graphic novel," with his series *A Contract with God* (1978). This form of story would break comic books out of just being about superheroes or cartoon characters. Recent examples of graphic novels translated to film are *Road To Perdition* (2002), which became an Oscar-nominated motion picture, *X-Men* (2000), *X-Men 2* (2003), and *From Hell* (2001).

Historical Events

Historical events have always been a great resource for film. Though period pieces are especially hard to set up because of the production expenses they may require, there is always room for a different perspective on history. Successful movies usually see history through an unexpected source rather than just an academic retelling of a tale. Years ago, movies were filled with "straight-on" biographies. Today, there has to be a different perspective or "take" on the subject matter or person. For example, the movie *Elizabeth* (1998), directed by Shekhar Kapur, was not just a retelling of the famous Queen's story but rather it was a mystery thriller that highlighted a forgotten fact about Queen Elizabeth—that more people wanted the young queen dead than alive, that there were traitors within her court, and that the young vivacious Elizabeth had to grow up very quickly in order to fill the shoes of the Queen of England. This also makes it very accessible to a modern audience because everyone can identify with having to become responsible and everyone can identify with betrayal and the loss of love and friendship.

Some movies will focus on specific storylines set against the backdrop of a big historical event. For example, the movie *Troy* (2004), directed by Wolfgang Petersen, told the tale from Achilles' point of view rather than the usual Helen/Paris or Hector angles, which relegated Achilles to a supporting character. While you can't tell the story of "Troy" without having Helen and Paris or Hector be a big part of that story, this "Troy" cashed in on the actor playing Achilles...Brad Pitt.

Some historical films, like Miramax's Oscar-winning *Shakespeare in Love* (1998), mix truth with fiction in an entertaining manner. Sometimes with these kinds of films, the writer may be researching something specific and out of that comes a totally different idea. We can't reiterate enough that you must think beyond what's just on the page.

Plays

Another source for material is from the theatre. Since the beginning of motion pictures, plays have consistently supplied the film business with material. Though these tend to be more character-driven dramas and currently seem to be less seen in motion picture theatres and more on cable and network television, plays usually offer a great showcase for actors. Sometimes, original plays, either workshopped or performed in small town repertory theatres, can also be a great resource of material for films.

Foreign language films remade into English language films

French, Korean, Spanish, German, Chinese, Japanese, and so on—foreign language films have had some major success stories when turned into English language films. The French film *The Unfaithful Wife* (1968) directed by Claude Chabrol became *Unfaithful* (2002) directed by Adrian Lyne, the Japanese film *Ringu* (1998) based upon KÔji Suzuki's book became *The Ring* (2002), and the Spanish film *Open Your Eyes* (1997) became *Vanilla Sky* (2001). These are just a few of the many foreign language films remade for the English language cinema. Some of these films may be obscure but offer a relatable idea that transcends language. Finding them is not as difficult as it may seem. Specialty video stores offer a wide array of foreign language films that may not have been released in the United States as theatrical motion pictures, yet are available on video or DVD from their original countries. Film Festivals also offer a wide variety of foreign language films, most of which do not receive theatrical distribution in the United States. Usually, the filmmakers are in attendance thereby making them very accessible to approach about obtaining rights to their films. Sometimes the more obscure a foreign film, the easier it is to get the English language rights. Through the course of film history, foreign movies have been a great inspiration for the American cinema and should not be overlooked today.

Remakes and Redos

While foreign language films make good remakes in English, some older films are also worthy of retelling. Although some might ask, "Why remake a film that was a success to begin with?" One must take into account a whole new generation who have not been exposed to those older movies along with the newest generation of actors wanting to tackle those juicy roles. Sometimes it's not just about remaking a film or even repeating a plotline, it's simply about reviving a memorable character and giving that character a whole new updated story. While some may argue which version of the movie is better, it would be better to look at remakes as individual pictures rather than make those comparisons. For example, *Ocean's Eleven* (1960) was an enjoyable movie that gave the studios an opportunity to put big stars together in an ensemble caper movie. 2001's version of *Ocean's Eleven* offered ensemble roles for some of the biggest stars of today and also was able to update the caper to a more technological age. Both were fun to watch and stand on their own as entertaining movies.

Recently, old television series have also unlocked more material for the big screen. People flocked to see *The Brady Bunch* (1995) and found it less like the series and more of a tongue-in-cheek version of the picture-perfect Brady family. It was still successful and offered up a sequel. *Bewitched* (2005) starring Nicole Kidman, *The Honeymooners* (2005) starring Cedric the Entertainer, and *Dukes of Hazzard* (2005) starring Jessica Simpson are just some of the recent television series/big screen translations, not to mention remakes of *Batman* (1989) and all its sequels, *Charlie's Angels* (2000) and its 2003 sequel, and *Mission: Impossible I—III* (1996, 2000, 2006 respectively). Remakes don't always guarantee success but more times than not it's worth the gamble because the built-in audience makes them more marketable.

Video Games

Computer games also offer development executives and writers a whole new world of storytelling. From these games, such movies as *Doom* (2005), *Lara Croft: Tomb Raider* (2001), and *Mortal Kombat* (1995) have emerged into larger than life movies, with some of them already franchises for more upcoming sequels.

SCREENWRITING COMPETITIONS

Screenwriting competitions are a dime a dozen. Every film festival seems to have one. In Chapter 13—"Resources" we discuss at length some of the top competitions. However, reading only the winners of these competitions shortchanges the development executive because many of the finalists and semi-finalists are worthy screenplays too. It is important to keep abreast of the competitions all over the world and learn which ones are the most reliable.

PITCHFESTS—THE NEW HOLLYWOOD

A number of organizations, film schools, and magazines offer a new way for writers to get their ideas into the Hollywood arena. "Pitchfests" is where a number of production companies, studio and/or network executives, and/or producers gather in a large room and writers have a chance to pitch their story ideas to each of them separately within three to five minutes (depending on the rules for each organization). Much like speed dating, a bell or signal is sounded and the writer moves on to the next table and another writer takes his or her place and the round starts again. This can be pretty exhausting to executives who are hearing pitch after pitch after pitch. Some of these pitch fests last the whole day or weekend, others are at two-hour stretches. The idea is to whet the executive's appetite enough to want to read the full screenplay. Usually, they will tell the writer if they're interested and either have them send the screenplay or treatment, or tell them to contact them so they can send a writer's release form prior to reading the material. Granted, there aren't any real statistics proving how successful speed pitching is or if any projects have made it to the screen, but it is another way to make contact for people who may not have agents or representation, and may not live in Hollywood, thereby making it harder to access industry people. Plus, where else can you pitch dozens of entertainment professionals all in one day?

UNDERLYING RIGHTS

If you have source material (i.e., a book, an article, a life story), there are rights that need to be obtained before pitching the story or putting pen to paper to develop the project. Sometimes the underlying rights negotiations can be quite complicated and will require a lawyer's input. There are many ways to go about obtaining the rights to an underlying source for a movie.

1) You can option the story and pay money for it. But, if you are just starting out, you may not be able to afford this. An option is an agreement which allows the producer or writer to have exclusive rights to that story for an outlined amount of time (usually a year) with possible extensions beyond that. Some stories, depending on how "in demand" they are, may only require a minimal option payment. We've optioned stories for one dollar because the rights owners saw the passion we had for the story and had faith in us to see the story through in a respectable way. Option agreements outline the amount and terms of payment should there be a development deal at a studio, production company, or television network.

2) Another way to obtain rights to a story is to get a letter signed by both parties authorizing the producer or writer exclusive rights to shop the story within a limited amount of time in order to get a development deal for it. The difference between this and an Option Agreement is that the rights owner can hold the producer or writer over a barrel upon setting up the project because the rights owner can turn the deal down if the money isn't enough or they're just not satisfied with the deal. Sometimes you can build a clause into this kind of an agreement that the owner of the rights must not turn down any reasonable offers comparable to such other deals within the industry.

Getting the rights to any underlying material requires a lawyer's help. Do not do this without an attorney or somewhere down the line when a deal is offered, you will run into problems because you didn't negotiate enough protection for yourself. A lawyer can help identify the areas that need to be covered, and make sure your interests are protected.

STARTING AN IDEA FILE

Every writer, producer, and development executive should have an idea file. Some drive around with a tape recorder so that they can capture any ideas or thoughts at any given moment.

Once you identify an article, a book, an idea, or any other underlying sources for material that can be adapted into film, there are several further questions you might ask yourself in order to back up your initial response to the story or concept. "Is this a movie I would pay to see?" "Does the story fill three acts—is there a beginning, middle, and an end?" "Are there enough compelling characters or can they be created to embellish the story?" Good stories are usually about someone trying to overcome something. So it is important to have conflict and obstacles in order for our main characters to try and overcome them (or not) and achieve the goals of the story. Some of the key questions to start asking are:

- *WHO* is the main character?
- *WHAT* is the premise of the story?
- *WHERE* does it take place?
- *WHEN* does it take place?
- *WHAT* does the main character want to achieve?
- *WHAT* will the character risk to get it?
- *HOW* does the story end?
- Think about the genre in which you're placing the story...is it a western, sci-fi, adventure, action, thriller?
- Reduce your story to a logline which will help you realize your premise.

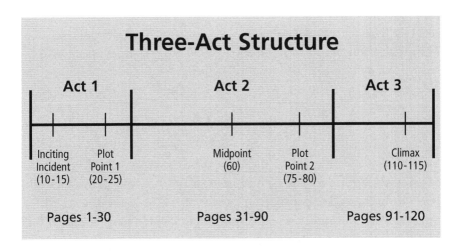

Three-Act Structure

Act 1	Act 2	Act 3
Inciting Incident (10-15) Plot Point 1 (20-25)	Midpoint (60) Plot Point 2 (75-80)	Climax (110-115)
Pages 1-30	**Pages 31-90**	**Pages 91-120**

- If you've gotten this far and you still like your story, now comes the time to fill in a paragraph on Act I, Act II, and Act III. Don't worry; you're not married to the initial ideas you put down. This is just to see if the story has *legs*, meaning will it fill up the three acts? It also helps to put down some of the important beats you want to see in the story and identify the possible turning points (see illustration on previous page).

THE IDEA FORM

So now you have all these ideas flowing out of your head with so many possibilities for stories. You can't just start pitching ideas everywhere; you have to have more than just a genre and an idea in your head; you have to be organized. Filling out this useful form (see next page) for each idea will not only help a writer, producer, or development executive structure the screenplay, but will also help if a writer or producer just wants to pitch the story. It's a great way to organize the idea and see if it truly is a movie. If you take your ideas and put them on paper using this format, you will have a file with lots of ideas, some of which you can start pitching right away while others can be revisited years later. There are many stories of producers who have pulled an idea from their file and sold it years after discovering it—because the timing was finally right, a piece of talent became interested, or enough time passed if there was a competing project. Ideas never die.

CONCLUSION

All through the ages, from Aristotle to Shakespeare, from George Polti to Lajos Egri, writers and teachers have debated how many plot lines exist in story. The human condition with all its turmoil has served for great drama and fodder for outstanding comedy over the centuries. Using similar plotlines, the characters and their tribulations are what differentiate each story. However, a story comes out of an idea, sometimes just a germ of an idea, and from that concept, a full-fledged narrative is developed. Ideas are everywhere and with today's technological age, there's no end to the depth of ideas found all over the world. Keeping an open and inquiring mind will only increase your chances of finding the basis for good stories.

By now, you are seeing ideas in everything you do and everything you see. Being able to flesh them out into detailed cinematic stories that turn into screenplays takes patience and perseverance. But it all starts with a thought or someone thinking out loud, "What would happen if..." We all have ideas. But do they translate to words and do those words become moving pictures? And if so, who will be interested in seeing them? These are the questions often asked when developing stories into screenplays. As a writer, director, development executive, or producer, you must lift every stone and open every door in order to find new and different tales to tell.

EXERCISE

Using the idea form, come up with your own idea from a magazine article. Write a page listing the project title, genre, logline, theme, hook ("gotcha"), and premise; first act, second act, and third act paragraphs—include turning points and climax.

Idea Form

EDWARDS / SKERBELIS ENTERTAINMENT

TITLE

GENRE:

PERIOD: LOCATION:

PREMISE:

THEME:

HOOK:

THE STORY:

ACT 1 (BEGINNING)

ACT II (MIDDLE)

ACT III (END)

11

"To Pitch Is a Bitch"

the art of pitching

Aside from lots of reading and networking, another thing you've hopefully learned so far in this book, is that you have to know how to pitch a story. You have to know how to whet people's appetites with a well-told tale. You have to know how to sell an idea. Writers alone are not the only ones selling their stories to Hollywood. Producers, development execs, agents, agents' assistants, development assistants, lawyers, even the waiter at your favorite restaurant, all have something to sell. It's important to be able to recognize a good story, pitch it succinctly, and, if you succeed, just maybe, you'll move up another rung on the already intimidating ladder of success in Hollywood. But pitching is not for everyone. One year, we were giving a full-day seminar on development to a writer's group in a neighboring state. Usually, at the end of the session, we let someone pitch us a story in front of everyone, then we critique the pitch, the story, and presentation. This particular time, two men got up and pitched us a thriller (usually not the easiest to pitch because you have to give a good deal of detail to drop clues and red herrings to build the suspense). Needless to say, the pitch did not go well. Our eyes glazed over, both of us trying to appear interested by nodding our heads every so often as if we were comprehending the throughline of the story which, of course, we were not. Finally, at the end, one of the writers came up to Rona and said that they were in the middle of writing the screenplay they just pitched us and could they submit it to her when it was done. Rona smiled and tried to nod graciously but her inner thought was, "Oh God, now I'm going to have to *read* another bad screenplay!" The script arrived and Rona read it. It became one of the movies she produced for television. The lesson here is "never judge a book by its cover." You may be a good writer and a lousy pitcher and sometimes quite the opposite. We intend to give you some basic tools and rules in order to learn how to pitch and make the most out of your story.

THINGS TO THINK ABOUT BEFORE PITCHING

1. *The "Gotcha" Line*: It's always good to use what we call the "Gotcha" line to begin a pitch. A "Gotcha" line is a marketing line, something you might see on a poster. For example, "The smartest man at Harvard turns out to be the janitor" or "This is the story of a Tom Clancy-like novelist who gets embroiled in what could be his own story. Now, instead of writing about it, he has to live it."

2. *Have a great logline*: It's short and sweet yet gives the essence of what the story is about. A simple one or two sentence logline goes a long way with a busy executive. They get the premise instantly and are now ready to hear your story. A good exercise is to come up with three loglines from some of your favorite movies—the more you practice, the more quickly you can come up with them. It's a great selling tool to master whether you're a story analyst, executive, producer, agent, or a writer. Here are some examples, we'll give you the logline, you tell us the movie (*answers on page 136*)

   - The picture perfect world of a 1950s suburban housewife comes crashing down after she discovers that her husband is gay.
   - True story of a female journalist, determined to change society in Dublin, who goes on a crusade to expose corrupt drug lords and their underworld with tragic results.

- An assassin, attacked on her wedding day by her boss and double-crossing husband-to-be, awakens from a four-year coma and seeks bloody revenge on her co-worker assassins and fiancé.
- A high-spirited young nun leaves her convent to care for seven children, bringing freedom and warmth to their strict household while unwittingly winning the heart of their cold father.
- When a nerdy high school student is bit by a spider, he turns into a web-slinging super hero. With his new defender of evil status, the teen learns that with great power comes great responsibility.
- A pirate pursues his nemesis across the Caribbean seas to regain control of his ship and break an ancient pirate curse with the blood of a beautiful virgin.

3. *Genre:* Be sure and say what genre your story is, i.e., comedy, drama, action/adventure, etc. Do not say, "This is a romantic/comedy/drama with some action/adventure set against a fantasy backdrop." Hollywood doesn't like to be confused. Hollywood likes things compartmentalized. It's more accessible that way. Even if your story has comedy and drama in it, don't say it's a drama when it's really a comedy with heartfelt moments. We had one person pitch us an action/adventure true life, dramatic comedy. Hmmm. That covers a lot but it doesn't give us any indication of what genre it is...in fact, it tells us that this story is all over the place. That's not to say that a drama can't have action or adventure. There are many films that cover more than one genre, but for the sake of the pitch, try to commit to as few as possible.

4. *The Length:* The pitch itself should be no longer than fifteen minutes. A word of advice: less is more! If you can get it down to ten minutes, that's even better. In that fifteen minutes *or less*, you should be able to convey the complete storyline, hitting on all the major beats, describing enough of the lead characters, and keeping the tone of your piece intact. Those major beats consist of the setup, the inciting incident, the first act turning point, the mid point, the second act turning point, the climax, and denouement. Know your Three Act Structure. It's been around since the beginning of storytelling and shouldn't be dismissed. We've already mentioned Aristotle's *Poetics.* His book is the oldest and most used book on the art of storytelling. Read it before you try to write another line.

You do not have to give every detail of every scene. It's tedious. Tell the throughline of the story and then sprinkle it with events along the way (not all the events, just the important ones that move the story forward). Be a storyteller. Make it interesting and appealing.

If the executive or producer has questions afterwards, you can fill in more of the blanks. You can also tell them, after they've heard the pitch, some of the great scenes you have in mind. In fact, you want to engage them in the development of your story in the room so they can see all the possibilities and potential your story has to offer. Better to do the pitch itself in less time and have time to explore more of the story and characters in a casual manner with the executive's input afterwards. By getting the executive involved in thinking about how to make the movie, finding out what he or she likes about it, what moments seem weak and how they might be fixed, may help convince the executive that your story might work for their studio. Granted, not all executives have the time to sit after a pitch meeting and brainstorm—usually that comes later when they've actually bought the material. However, if you can get them to think about all the elements while you're in the room, then they may continue to think about it after you leave. Remember, this is a collaborative business. Getting the development executive on board early, making suggestions, and contributing to the creative process can't hurt the possibility of a sale.

There was one story told to us by a creative executive about a vice president at a major studio who happened to be one of the nicest, well-respected executives at that studio. One day, she and another lower level creative executive sat and listened to a writer pitch...and pitch...and pitch... his story. After a painful hour went by, the writer declared, "...and that's the end of my first act." Needless to say, that executive didn't bother to stick around to hear the rest of the pitch. In fact, as the story goes, the executive laughed out loud uncontrollably and stated to everyone at the meeting that she could no longer listen to anymore and had heard enough. Gee, what are the chances of that pitch being bought? We can't stress enough to keep your pitch to no more than fifteen minutes and above all, keep it simple, concise, entertaining, and compelling. It can be done.

5. *Describe the characters* as they're introduced, briefly, but enough so the executive and/or producer gets who they are and where they come from and maybe where they are going. Give your main characters names and allude to their ages if necessary. Giving ages can help the executive visualize who might be right for the part.

6. *Describe some of the moments.* If it's a comedy, make sure you have some comic moments in your pitch, if it's an action piece, make sure you describe some of the action set pieces (not all of them), without encumbering your pitch with too much verbiage. Keep it simple.

7. *Resolve your storyline and end the pitch.* Make sure you end the pitch. We've seen writers who kind of "fade out" their pitch. It's much better to declare "...and that's the end of the story" then just letting your last remaining moment of the story linger without end. After the pitch, the executive and/or producer might have some comments. They may have a question or two. Be prepared to come up with the answers.

8. *Practice* in front of the mirror, make it interesting and exciting rather than a recitation. You might say to yourself, "I'm in a room, not a lecture hall." Use different tonal qualities in your voice to help accentuate certain aspects of the story so the telling of it doesn't drone on in monotone. There is a well-known lecturer's trick: if people look like they're glazing over, falling asleep, or losing interest, you can raise your voice slightly to grab the audience's attention back again. We've been in a small room with an executive and her "creative executive," who sat behind her. He began to nod off, his eyes rolling to the back of his head, even though the writer was pitching his story beautifully. The executive didn't see him dozing, but the rest of us did. It was very disconcerting. He must have had a sleepless night, staying up reading all those spec scripts that came in—or maybe it was too much networking!

   Some people pitch using index cards to refer to during the meeting. This is quite acceptable as long as you are not so married to the cards that you lose all eye contact with the person you're pitching to. It's always better to memorize and pitch more casually to the executive. But if you feel you need to have those cards to refer to, practice using them so you barely look at them, always keep the focus on the story and the person you are pitching it to, since that person is the one who makes the decision to move forward with your pitch—or not. If there are two people in the room, share some of that eye contact with the other executive so that he, too, is engaged in the story—especially if that person is taking notes as you pitch. If you don't make that connection with the executive, you've most likely lost your shot at selling him your story.

9. *The hook* should be given in the first few minutes of your pitch, or in the logline to start your pitch. The hook is the crux of the story. Below are some examples of hooks. Can you guess the movie? (*answers on page 136*)

   * A guy known for cooling good luck to those at the gambling tables loses his knack and becomes lucky.
   * A lawyer has to tell the truth for twenty-four hours.
   * The clash of western and eastern military cultures collide in 19th Century Japan.

10. *Know your executives/production companies.* Make sure the person you are pitching to is responsive to the kind of material you are pitching, i.e., don't pitch a WWII drama to a person who loves comedies, or pitch a science fiction piece to someone who doesn't like science fiction. The same goes for production companies. If a production company is known for big action movies, think twice about pitching them a low budget indie film. You just wouldn't pitch an edgy, dark, adult, action film to Nickelodeon Pictures.

ORGANIZING YOUR PITCH

A good way to organize your thoughts for the pitch is by writing it out using the idea form illustrated in Chapter 10—"Finding Ideas." This invaluable form can be used for any number of thoughts and ideas. Should you find an article, a song, even a hint of an idea, you can enter it on this form, and start creating a story from it. You can use it to break down an existing script's structure. You can use it to help you practice the pitch for your story. Once you write these story ideas down, you'll discover that you've now created an "idea" file. We all keep "idea" files. Development execs, writers, and producers are known for taking a snippet of an article and creating a whole movie based upon a concept from that article. We cut out articles, watch news programs, see something happen in real life we make a note of, etc., and we throw them into this file for safekeeping for the future. When we are at a loss for an idea, we go to that file, and start sifting through the many ideas we've kept and saved, hoping that one will trigger a new potential project. Congratulations! This is the beginning of your "idea" file!

CONCLUSION

Remember that executives, agents, and producers have already heard hundreds and hundreds of pitches—and that's just this month! Also, most producers, writers, and agents think they have the one script or pitch that outshines every other piece of material out there. Sometimes they do, but most times they don't. How do you set yourself apart from all the others? How do you make your story heard? Well, for one thing, if you have the pitch meeting set up, you're already one step ahead of the game. You have your chance to set yourself apart from all the others out there pitching their wares because you have their full attention, face to face. Have an understanding that while you have their attention, you must make the most of it because you won't have their attention for very long. This is your fifteen minutes of fame, as Andy Warhol would say. The question is, will you get an extension of that fame?

EXERCISE

Take the article you created a story from in the last chapter and practice a fifteen minute pitch based upon that article. Use the Idea Form to help organize your pitch.

ANSWERS TO LOGLINES: *Far from Heaven*; *Veronica Guerin*; *Kill Bill V. I and II*; *The Sound of Music*; *Spiderman*; and *Pirates of the Caribbean: The Curse of the Black Pearl*.

ANSWERS TO HOOKS: *The Cooler*; *Liar, Liar*; *The Last Samurai*.

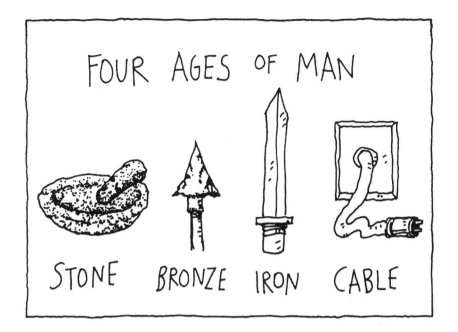

FOUR AGES OF MAN

STONE BRONZE IRON CABLE

12

"Surfing Channels"

crossing over into television and cable movies

Up till now, we've been discussing the development of movies with a bent towards the feature film arena, but we would be remiss not to talk about made-for-television movies.

Since the beginning of television history, movies have been a staple on television. However, the original film strictly made-for-television came much later and covered a large array of subjects. Original movies made-for-television could be programmers or prestige projects. Usually, they focused on issues (both political and personal) that the audience could identify with. They have been used to educate, inform, and in some cases, like *The Burning Bed* (1984), can focus on challenging themes, instigating action by legislators and organizations, and helping those who may be in similar situations. *The Burning Bed*, based on the true story of Francine Hughes, was about a battered Michigan housewife who was prosecuted in 1977 for dousing her abusive husband with gasoline and setting him on fire as he slept. It was one of the first TV movies to be "ripped from the headlines," and is still shown today at battered women's shelters around the world. This was not an easy movie to get made. Anne Carlucci was director of development for Norman Lear at the time. The networks usually had commitment deals with stars and she knew in order to get this movie made she needed to attach one such star. She suggested Farrah Fawcett who had just signed a talent deal with NBC. Her gamble paid off. *The Burning Bed's* impact proved that movies made-for-television could shed a light on difficult subject matter and the audience wouldn't run from it. Instead, they tuned in and continue to do so. There are countless other movies made-for-television that have also serviced the public by not only enlightening them but also engaging them.

DIFFERENCES BETWEEN STUDIOS AND NETWORKS

First off, it should be understood that television programs unlike studio feature films are advertiser driven, that means that in order to air any programming on television (other than premium pay cable networks like HBO and Showtime), the networks must sell a certain amount of commercial spots to pay for the programming. How successful the show is will determine the cost of the advertising spots. This is where ratings come in. If a show has a high Nielsen rating, it will rate better ad revenues. That is why a show like *Friends* could afford to pay their stars such high salaries. It was a highly rated show and therefore demanded higher ad fees.

The other thing to understand about television is that it needs to fill up its programming schedule. Unlike feature films, the networks can't have dead air. A studio can make as much or as little product as they deem necessary and affordable for profitability. A network must fill the airtime and most networks air programming twenty-four hours a day, seven days a week.

The amount of commercial time was originally regulated via The National Association of Broadcaster's Code (NAB Code). At that time, the networks had a limited amount of advertising spots to sell per show. A half-hour show could have four minutes of commercials, while an hour show was allowed eight minutes. A two-hour movie was allowed sixteen minutes of advertising time. However, in 1982, the code was deemed unconstitutional and a violation of the Sherman Anti-Trust Act, especially since it limited how many ads a television program could air, constituting a restraint of trade, and, thereby, manipulating the cost of commercial time. With the government's deregulating-mania at the time, the code was abandoned and the broadcasters thought they would have more flexibility and more opportunity to program their shows better. All it really amounted to was reducing the actual program content and add to the amount of commercials on the air. On average and depending on the network, a half-hour show has seven and a half to eight minutes of commercials with a show running twenty-two to twenty-two and a half minutes long while an hour show runs forty-two minutes with eighteen minutes of commercials. A two-hour movie now runs twenty-eight minutes of commercial advertising leaving the programming content to a slim ninety-two minutes. However, some networks have reduced the content to eighty-eight minutes, broadcasting thirty-two minutes of advertising!

However, that being said, you can still develop good movies within that time frame, and impact the airwaves with compelling stories that raise the consciousness of the public.

ORIGINS OF THE MADE-FOR-TELEVISION MOVIE

In the beginning, networks like NBC, ABC, and later CBS had regular movie nights showing feature length films that they licensed from the studios. Throughout the history of television, movies were still the networks' highest rated programming. With the premiere of *The Million Dollar Movie* in 1955, it was pretty clear to the powers that be that movie fans would stay home to watch a re-showing of one of their favorite films rather than go out to a movie theatre. Hollywood studios licensed their pre-1948 titles to television, which were mostly black and white and worked perfectly for the then black and white televisions in living rooms across America. However, with the advent of color TV becoming more of a reality, the networks wanted newer films, especially NBC, which had a lot invested in color technology. Beginning with the 1961-1962 season, NBC premiered in prime time, *Saturday Night at the Movies* which telecast newer movies. The ratings went through the roof and the two other major networks soon followed suit. Soon after, screenings of recent Hollywood movies became standard fare on television. Nearly 40 percent of all television sets tuned into Alfred Hitchcock's *The Birds* in 1968, just five years after its release. Half the nation's television sets tuned into *Gone With the Wind* (1939) when it was shown in two parts in 1976.

By the late 1960s, however, it became clear that there were too many movies showing on network television and not enough films coming out of the studio pipeline. That, coupled with Hollywood studios charging higher and higher prices for TV screenings of their precious features, caused network executives to seek another potential product: original movies made-for-television.

It is important to point out that the made-for-television movie celebrated its 50th anniversary in 2004. The first original TV movie, *See How They Run*, aired on NBC in 1964 and starred John Forsythe. Executive Grant Tinker, pushed NBC to make more original films and get rid of those pre-1948 feature films they were showing. Originally, *The Killers* (1964), directed by Don Siegel and exhibiting Ronald Reagan's last acting performance, was developed to be the first television movie. It was jointly produced by NBC and Universal Pictures and paved the way in the formatting of this genre. However, it was deemed too violent for home viewing and instead was released as a feature film in theatres.

Another pivotal moment in the history of television movies was when NBC contracted with Lew Wasserman's MCA's Universal Studios (ironic, since now they are one and the same) to create a regular series of world premiere movies made-for-television, thus making the made-for-television movie a fixture on TV sets across the country. NBC was the frontrunner when it came to television movies. However, ABC, being dead last in the ratings race had nothing to lose. So in 1969, producer Roy Huggins pitched a "way out idea" to a young executive named Barry Diller, who was then head of prime time programming at the "alphabet" network. Huggins' idea was to have a slot that would play original made-for-television movies on a weekly basis. Thus, premiered the ABC *Movie of the Week* in which all the movies shown would be originals. The gamble turned out to be a huge success with the ABC *Tuesday Night Movie* coming in fifth place for the 1971-72 season. It became the gold standard for movies made-for-television. Other networks, seeing how successful ABC's movie of the week was, jumped on the bandwagon and thus the slang term "MOW" was born.

TV movies dared to shed light on subject matter that wasn't always dealt with in feature films. Social and political issues were often reduced to a personal story of one character's journey—thereby making the subject matter more accessible to audiences. Movies made-for-television had the courage to talk about AIDS as early as 1985 with *An Early Frost* (NBC), homosexuality in *That Certain Summer* (1972-ABC), racism and civil rights in *The Autobiography of Jane Pittman* (1974-CBS), Alzheimers in *Do You Remember Love?* (1984-CBS), rape in *A Case of Rape*, (1974-NBC), incest in *Something about Amelia* (1984-ABC), growing up with hearing impaired parents in *Love is Never Silent* (1985-NBC), and schizophrenia in *Promise* (1986-CBS). TV movies began to earn praise as well; the "alphabet" network earned five Emmys, a celebrated George Foster Peabody award, and citations from the NAACP and the American Cancer Society for an airing of *Brian's Song* in 1972.

Movies made-for-television sometimes offered actors juicier roles than feature films, required less time to film it, and sometimes even catapulted an episodic television actor or actress into the realm of "serious actor" as *Sybil* (1976-NBC) did for Sally Field or *A Case of Rape* did for Elizabeth Montgomery. These two actresses would no longer be just considered sitcom actresses anymore thanks to the television movie. Field's career even crossed over into feature films (winning two Academy awards) after that along with other such noteworthy actors as James Caan (*Brian's Song),* James Woods (*Promise*), Glenn Close (*Something About Amelia*), and many others.

Made-for-television movies were also a good way for the networks to try out stories and characters as "backdoor pilots," meaning the movie might end up becoming a series if the ratings warranted it. Movies like *Bracken's World* (1969), *Then Came Bronson* (1969), and *Fame is the Name of The Game* (1966), were all movies made-for-television prior to becoming series. *The Homecoming: A Christmas Story* (1971) became *The Waltons*. Dramatic series such as *The Blue Knight, Ironside, Night Gallery*, and *Police Story*, were all made-for-television movies first and later became series.

Along side television movies came the "mini-series," also masterminded by ABC with *Rich Man Poor Man* airing as the first mini-series in 1976. But it was ABC's *Roots* (1977) that changed the dynamics of the TV movie and the mini-series. It proved that an audience would stay tuned for eight consecutive nights and broke what would be considered box office records, scoring an estimated 130 million households tuning into at least one of those nights. Eighty million people watched the final episode. Nowhere can you get those kinds of results in the feature film world. Executives realized that they had an event on their hands that could equal in ad revenues what any feature film could. Thus the "event" movie was born. NBC followed suit with *Holocaust* (1978) and *Shogun* (1980), while ABC presented *The Thorn Birds* (1983) and *The Winds of War* (1983) followed by its sequel *War and Remembrance* (1988). CBS contributed *Lonesome Dove* (1989).

As stated, television is in the business of selling advertising to pay for their shows. If a movie captures a vast audience, the network ad revenues increase and the networks make more money.

The Winds of War aired on six successive February evenings, for a total of eighteen hours at a cost of production of nearly $40 million. This mini-series shot over 200 days, from a script of nearly 1000 pages, starred "real" movie stars Robert Mitchum and Ali McGraw, and had a very prestigious cast based upon a very successful novel. It had a built-in audience...but if it hadn't been good, it still would have lost its audience after the first night. It more than returned its sizable cost by capturing half the total viewing audience and selling out all its advertising spots at $300,000 per minute. This is just one example of how the business of television works.

Mini-series have always been event programming, much like the summer blockbusters or tentpole feature releases in the movie theatres. They're usually based upon books, true-life stories or events, and air over at least two or more nights.

In the 80s, the TV movie was in full force, sometimes airing three times a week on one network. There was an over-abundance of potboilers, disease of the week, and social issues to cover.

However, the marketplace began to change. HBO entered the scene and drew a huge audience to its uncut, uninterrupted presentation of movies. Home video was also spreading and suddenly feature films were not as valuable on network television, especially when film fans could watch their favorite theatrical films any time they wanted without commercial interruption. The networks needed to fill up their programming schedules and they did so with made-for-television movies.

Even HBO decided to introduce original programming into their schedule by producing original movies with "stunt" casting, meaning they enticed big stars with juicy parts. The first such movie starred Robert Duval in *The Terry Fox Story* (1983), an inspirational tale about an athlete who ran a 3,000 mile marathon across Canada after losing a leg to cancer. This was followed by a second star-studded movie, *Between Friends* (1983), starring Elizabeth Taylor and Carol Burnett. In the beginning, HBO knew that in order to gain a subscriber audience, they needed to lure big stars to wrest viewers away from the major networks.

Ten years later, it was *The Positively True Adventures of the Alleged Texas Cheerleader-Murdering Mom* (1993), based on the true story of a

Texas mom (Holly Hunter) who tried to hire a hitman to kill off her daughter's cheerleading competition, as well as the competitor's mother, that branded HBO as a leader in original made-for-television movies. Screenwriter Jane Anderson's "take" was to make this true but outrageous story a dark comedy—setting in motion a tone for the pay TV network and a whole new era of made-for-television movies that had a slightly different angle than the straight ahead network movies previously seen on the tube. It won the Cable Ace, the DGA, and the Emmy for its writer and stars, and was a defining moment for the pay cable network. HBO raised the bar to what's possible for movies made-for-television, following up this movie with such prestigious and Emmy Award-winning projects as *And The Band Played On* (1993) starring Mathew Modine, *Truman* (1995) starring Gary Sinese, and Don *King: Only In America* (1997) starring Ving Rhames. Now, not only did viewers turn to HBO for original programming, but they could also watch their favorite theatrical movies uncut and without interruption. This truly slashed into advertising revenues for the networks. Nowadays, networks have to work harder to find an audience and do so by the packaging of bigger stars and more event-like original movies.

Thanks to Grant Tinker for pushing the made-for-television movie onto the primetime schedule, Lew Wasserman and Universal Television for actually producing them, and Barry Diller for programming the Movie of the Week (MOW), television movies have become a staple for all the networks, though lately they are programming them less and less. As of this printing, there aren't any networks running a regular movie night anymore. With the advent of reality television, Cable is the new home for scripted television and most notably the original made-for-television movie.

MOVIES MADE-FOR-TELEVISION TODAY

Entering the 21st century, the television movie lost its footing. But like everything else in Hollywood, it's cyclical. For a number of years, the one-hour drama was a hard sell, now they're a network staple (thanks to *Law & Order* and *CSI* spinoffs), along with reality television, in network primetime. Comedies are at an all time low on the schedules and made-for-television movies are not as prevalent. With cable networks like the Hallmark Channel and Lifetime, made-for-television movies continue to thrive, sometimes airing one original movie or more a month. Some of the smaller networks on cable are also trying their hand with programming a few original movies a year. However, a great story that has a personal journey set against a larger backdrop, whether it's an issue or an event, will always find a home on television. It's a matter of knowing your buyers and what they are looking for. Each network tries to differentiate itself from the others by being very specific as to whom their target audience is. A good example of this would be Lifetime or Oxygen, which markets quite specifically to the female market. MTV markets to an under 18-crowd, while CBS has always skewed older, though that is changing too. Knowing the marketplace, the audience, and the network's mandate will help in determining what kind of movie they may or may not buy. As with feature films, it is important to know your buyer!

THE SEVEN-ACT AND EIGHT-ACT STRUCTURE

The television movie structure differs from the feature film three-act structure in that, with the exception of HBO, Showtime, and other commercial free broadcasters, there are commercial breaks to be considered. Therefore, made-for-television movies are configured mostly in a *seven-act* structure, allowing for seven commercial breaks. However, a number of broadcasters have instituted an *eight-act* structure to accommodate even more advertising time. That being said, a feature film written in its traditional three acts can often still be translated to a seven or eight-act structure.

The Act Break

At the end of each act break should be a cliffhanger—a hook that will bring the audience back after the commercial to find out what happens. It can be suspenseful, a heavy dramatic moment or bring out the conflicts between the characters and/or the situations. In particular, Act One and Act Three are your most crucial act breaks. Act One typically sets up the story and its characters with an inciting incident. It also establishes the potential obstacles in the character's journey. Different networks like different first act lengths. Generally, they are around twenty minutes—in the case of Court TV and Lifetime, they may be up to twenty-eight minutes. Act Three should have a turning point—a crisis point that propels the story in a surprising direction thereby, once again, luring the audience back, and hopefully preventing them from channel surfing during the commercial break. The Act Three break is the hour break and usually comes five minutes on either side of the hour, not directly on the hour. Act Five would be comparable to the end of Act Two in a feature film. The last two acts would include the climax and resolution of the story, as would

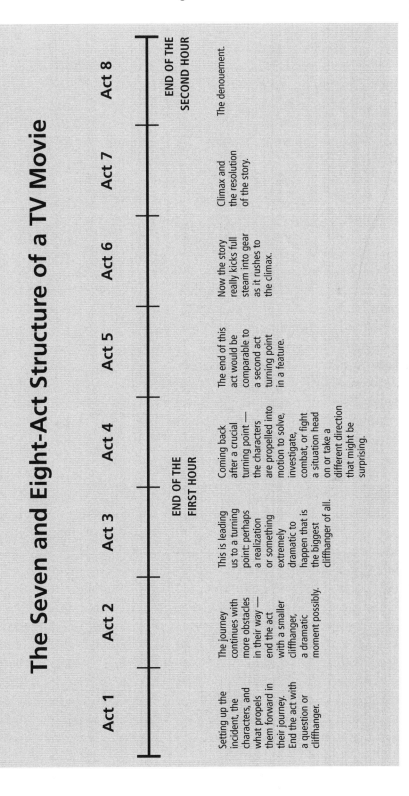

The Seven and Eight-Act Structure of a TV Movie

Act 1	Act 2	Act 3	Act 4	Act 5	Act 6	Act 7	Act 8

END OF THE FIRST HOUR

END OF THE SECOND HOUR

Act 1: Setting up the incident, the characters, and what propels them forward in their journey. End the act with a question or cliffhanger.

Act 2: The journey continues with more obstacles in their way — end the act with a smaller cliffhanger, a dramatic moment possibly.

Act 3: This is leading us to a turning point; perhaps a realization or something extremely dramatic to happen that is the biggest cliffhanger of all.

Act 4: Coming back after a crucial turning point — the characters are propelled into motion to solve, investigate, combat, or fight a situation head on or take a different direction that might be surprising.

Act 5: The end of this act would be comparable to a second act turning point in a feature.

Act 6: Now the story really kicks full steam into gear as it rushes to the climax.

Act 7: Climax and the resolution of the story.

Act 8: The denouement.

the third act of a feature. It is not about the page count for each act aside from Act One and Act Three; the story can be broken up into commercial breaks according to the drama that's on the screen. It would look something like the illustration on the previous page. However, in the case of the eight-act structure, some networks break up the climax so there's a double cliffhanger and then there's a short tag or wrap up after the commercial break following the climax.

THE DEVELOPMENT TEAM IN TELEVISION MOVIES

For the past thirty years, the development team in television has resembled a skeleton version of the studio's feature creative development team. Television is not as top heavy, usually having one head of movies and mini-series who reports directly to the president of the network. Under that head, there may be two to four development executives (usually called directors of development or vice presidents) who do nothing but work with producers and writers in developing movies for television. They report to the head of movies and mini-series. The same would be true for drama and comedy development executives who develop and oversee episodic television.

Prior to the 70s, however, programming executives scheduled the many different types of fare seen on television. As a number of programs were sponsored by corporations such as Hallmark (who still actively sponsors two-hour network movie specials to this day) or Chrysler Corporation, not only did they pay for the programming, but they also bought up all the commercial time in "their" time slot. Those corporations had a strong hand in the types of programs that were aired. When Universal made that historic deal with NBC for a series of original movies, they paid for the production and NBC paid a licensing fee to Universal, plus sold ad revenue to help pay for the time slot. As networks moved more into controlling their airtime by either producing their own original programming or buying product from studios and other production companies, we have seen less and less corporate sponsored programming.

While there are still programming executives, a new executive emerged to help develop the vast amount of original programming the networks were offering. Today, those executives take pitch meetings, read writing samples, watch dailies, and perform a lot of the same functions as a studio executive does on a feature film. However, with television movies, it is easier to sell a well thought out pitch or truth-based story than it is in feature films. Nevertheless, while fewer development executives are needed, relative to the studio system, their plates are quite full as they oversee the many movies in development—even though only a handful may get made.

GENERATING IDEAS FOR TELEVISION MOVIES

Finding new ideas for made-for-television movies is not much different than finding ideas for feature films. The difference is that the budget is much smaller and certain ideas lend themselves better to the big screen rather than to the box. A huge special effects-driven movie translates better on a movie screen than it does on a television screen, though lately, a network might take a chance on a mini-series encompassing feature-like effects such as *The Mists of Avalon* (2001) or *Steven Spielberg Presents Taken* (2002). As feature films tend to be about how much money they might gross their initial weekends, the television movie is about ratings—finding stories that have a marketable edge, a timeliness, and compelling drama with watchable stars that will appeal to a mass audience helps capture these ratings. Magazines, newspapers, and even magazine format television shows such as *60 Minutes*, have all contributed great stories for original movies made-for-television. Identifying those stories that might draw an audience to watch that particular movie above all the other choices on television is key to being a successful television movie producer or television development executive.

CONCLUSION

Television is a different animal from the feature film world. While the networks are interested in high ratings, they also are able to do smaller and more compelling dramas that are no longer suitable for the big screen because the box office doesn't seem to warrant it, unfortunately. TV movie roles can attract a higher caliber of talent these days because there is less character-driven material in feature films to exhibit an actor's talent in the way that television movies offer. Though earning quite a bit less than they might from a feature film, an actor also spends far less time filming a TV movie than he or she would a feature film. The average TV movie shoots in less than twenty days—some even do it in seventeen days—compared to three to six months often required for shooting a feature film.

Not every story translates into a movie made-for-television. For example, rarely do you see comedic films, though romantic comedies do occasionally appear. Historically, comedies don't usually translate to big ratings on the small screen. This might be due to the fact that there is no "laugh track," so viewers might find themselves laughing alone. Hearing the laughter of others, albeit in a movie theatre or on a sitcom, is infectious. Sitting alone and watching a comedic movie may inhibit laughter. Regardless, these movies tend to lose in the ratings game. Stories that translate well to the small screen have an intimacy, a more personal story...something identifiable for an audience to grab onto or enlighten an area of life that not only educates but entertains. Books that are sagas, and needing more than two hours to chronicle, may be better suited to a miniseries than a theatrical motion picture. Thrillers, especially from a female perspective, also might find a home in the television movie.

Development, whether it's a feature film or a made-for-television movie, is still a collaboration of storytelling—trying to convey it in a dramatic way is the goal in either medium.

EXERCISE 1

Take the pitch outline you did from the magazine article, which was in a three-act structure, and break it down into seven acts.

EXERCISE 2

Watch a MOW (Movie of the Week) and pay attention to how the story develops at each of the commercial breaks.

13

resources

We have always been believers in having books, and even more books, of reference data and information on our bookshelves. It wasn't so long ago when that was the normal protocol of research for compiling lists, whether talent lists, credit lists, contact lists, etc., etc. However, today with technology at our fingertips, a vast amount of information once tediously researched and uncovered via libraries and countless reference books, is now available in the space of a few minutes with the click of a button.

Information is golden and the more you know and compile, whether on paper or in your brain, the more it will help you with your projects, jobs and finding jobs, and just being on top of the latest development tools and resources. The following is just the tip of the iceberg, but we hope it will be helpful to you in your work.

MOVIES

One of the best resources you can find is studying the great movies that have already been made. Today, there are wonderful collections of early films, that can be rented or purchased on DVD, that are the very foundation of our contemporary cinema, including *The Movies Begin: A Treasury of Early Cinema*—featuring films of Edwin S. Porter, Thomas A. Edison, Louis Lumiere, George Melies, etc. from Film Preservation Associates (1994). Those early days highlight the origins and continuing development of the motion picture story. DVDs usually offer more historical facts by providing the director's, writer's, and actors' commentaries on the process of making the film. We can't stress enough how important it is to learn about great storytelling from some of the great storytellers in cinematic history. Renting DVDs directed by such celebrated filmmakers and screenwriters as George Cukor, Frank Capra, Billy Wilder, John Huston, Martin Scorsese, Steven Spielberg, Dalton Trumbo, Steve Zaillian, Waldo Salt, Ernest Lehman, and countless others is an education in itself. Keeping up with current films is also extremely valuable. It will help you generate new lists of writers, actors, and directors to add to your "favorites" lists. Even seeing *bad* movies will help you see the pitfalls that should be avoided in your own work. There's a lesson in everything!

REFERENCE BOOKS

With so many books claiming to be the "end all" of reference books, there are a few that are truly helpful and deserve to be recognized. One of the most useful is the *Hollywood Creative Directory*. Listing almost all the production companies, studios, television and cable networks, along with their staff members and phone numbers, this one-stop-shopping tome should be the first on anyone's list who is serious about succeeding in any aspect of the entertainment industry. They also list production companies with deals as well as a few of their credits. This book is one of the first books we recommend to "up and comers" and seasoned professionals alike. The Hollywood Creative Directory also publishes *The Hollywood Representation Directory* listing all the agents, managers, and attorneys; it's another valuable resource to have on your bookshelf. The directories are also available online in a subscription database.

The Directors Guild of America (DGA) and the Producers Guild of America (PGA) have directories for sale to the public, listing their members and contact information. The Writers Guild of America (WGA) and The Screen Actors Guild (SAG) have "agency" departments that you can call and ask who represents the talent. These directories are important tools when you are compiling a talent list or wish to find out who represents talent, which then leads to finding out if they are available to do your movie.

The WGA, SAG, and the DGA also have printed booklets listing their "schedule of minimums"—the negotiated theatrical and television basic agreement between the guilds and the studios. It is important to have this information if you are doing a union movie and need to know the basic minimum salaries and fringes that need to be paid to your talent. These agreements list every possible scenario from documentaries to variety shows, from TV series to theatrical films and the corresponding fees that need to be paid in order to meet guild minimums.

Since 1937, the Academy of Motion Picture Arts & Sciences has offered the *Academy Players Directory*. This bible for casting directors as well as agents and managers is an encyclopedia of actors. Now offered online as well for a very reasonable yearly price for industry professionals, this is probably the most useful tool when it comes to casting. Actors pay a yearly fee to be included in the bi-annual editions of the *Players Directory*, which includes the yearly online service.

TRADE PAPERS

In order to know on a day-to-day basis what's going on in the industry, you must read the trade papers which detail scripts that have been sold, deals that have been made, weekly production charts, executive shuffles, the latest entertainment news, film, television, stage, and music reviews. You don't necessarily need to get both trades, but it is imperative to be reading at least one. *The Hollywood Reporter* and *Daily Variety* are the kingpins of the industry trade papers. Established in 1905, Variety also offers a weekly and an international version as well as a Gotham version with up-to-the-minute news for the East Coast. Recently, Variety has launched a Chinese language edition (the first time it's been published in any language other than English), servicing Asia.

One of the most valuable articles published twice a year in *Daily Variety* is *Facts on Pacts*, listing all the production companies with term deals at all the major and mini-major studios. Again, this is helpful in targeting projects to specific producers with deals at specific studios.

The Hollywood Reporter has been in existence for over seventy-five years. Started in 1930 by William R. "Billy" Wilkerson, it was known as being rather aggressive and opinionated in its early days, a renegade news tome to compete with the more stalwart *Variety*. Aside from the normal entertainment news and features, today's *Hollywood Reporter* profiles a list of literary sales once a month called *Literary Hollywood*—projects optioned and/or purchased by studios, networks, and production companies. This is a valuable resource for knowing who is buying what and the kinds of movies that are being developed.

The Hollywood Reporter offers an in-depth production chart in that it includes the genres of the films in production, pre-production, or development. *The Hollywood Reporter* also has a Gotham version, distributed in a PDF format.

Both papers are published five days a week with up-to-the-minute news. Both have Web sites that, if you're a subscriber, you can search the archives for past articles or if you're not a subscriber, check out the headlines. Both offer special editions—bonus issues—on various aspects of the business including Award shows (i.e., Oscar, Emmy, Golden Globe), independent film, film festival issues, film and TV music, etc. Finally both offer the headlines in a free daily e-mail.

A new weekly trade paper on the scene is *Television Week*, which offers readers in-depth news on anything to do with television and cable, including ratings, deals, and new technology.

In order to track books that are coming out, *Publisher's Weekly*, published weekly, and *Kirkus Review*, published twice a month, offers reviews of books prior to their publication dates and sometimes up to three months in advance. Both have extensive Web sites and the *Kirkus* offers a free newsletter via e-mail. These are pricier publications but they are of great use if books play into your development slate.

The Hollywood Reporter—Literary Sales Sample

TITLE	SOURCE	WRITER	BUYER	DISTRIBUTOR	TERMS/PRICE	GENRE
Ahab's Wife	Novel	Helena Kriel	Camelot Pictures	n/a	Low-six	Drama
Arthur C. Clarke's Venus Prime	Book	Auth. Paul Preuss	WatWorks	n/a	n/a	Thriller
Before	Pitch	Niell Johnson	Mostow/Lieberman Prods.	n/a	Mid-six	Thriller
The Blessed Virgins	Spec script	Sarah Kelly	Maverick Film Co.	n/a	n/a	Comedy-drama
Fat Man	Spec script	Mike Reise	Columbia Pictures	Sony	$875K	Comedy

ONLINE RESOURCES

With the advent of the Internet, there are some nifty Web sites and systems one can use that will save you an enormous amount of research time and effort. One of the industry standards is StudioSystem (www.studiosystemsinc.com) utilized by most of the studios themselves and some of the more prominent production companies. StudioSystem merged with Baseline/FilmTracker in 2004 to form Baseline StudioSystems. They offer tools for production companies and studios to manage internal searches of coverage, competitive development projects, and film and TV industry contacts. They have up-to-the-minute databases on what's in development and where, which executive is in charge of the project, credits, status, etc. You can create talent lists from their database as well as view studio production slates, box office reports, development reports, and more.

FilmTracker (www.filmtracker.com), also part of the Baseline StudioSystems family, is another in-depth and verified info database available to anyone for various flat monthly fee packages (priced differently for studios vs. individuals). It also offers filmmakers and development execs a number of other things like tracking boards and a load of discussion groups pertaining to all kinds of genres and jobs in the industry.

Within StudioSystem is housed Script Log—a customized log of submissions and project drafts—that can create coverage reports instantly. "In Hollywood" is the third part of StudioSystem where you can find film start and wrap information with a personal tracker for updates on films. However, as good as this sounds, StudioSystem is incredibly expensive for an individual and, therefore, is used only by the studios or the more prominent independent production companies and agencies, though they do offer a consumer rate without all the bells and whistles.

The Internet Movie Database (www.IMDB.com) is a free Web site where you can look up movies and their complete credit list via a comprehensive database. You can also look up individuals. For a small monthly stipend, you can join The Internet Movie Database Pro Web site (www.IMDBPRO.com), which also offers a directory database of companies, talent representation, in production charts, box office grosses, and more.

Screen Actors Guild offers a separate Web site (www.castsag.com) where you can find out an actor's representation. Though it seems limited to agency representation, it is a free service and a good place to start. Another great source for finding out who represents talent is Who

Represents? (www.whorepresents.com—no jokes, please!). This Web site offers a vast database matching talent with their agents and/or managers. Some guilds will only allow three names to be looked up in their agency department at a time via the phone, so Who Represents? can save you time and fingernails from redialing the guilds to find out who represents the fifteen people on your potential talent list. This is a fee-based Web site offering a choice of both a monthly and yearly fee.

SUGGESTED READING

While there are many books written to help the writer, producer, director, and future development executive, we'd like to suggest a few books to have on your bookshelf. These books will help sustain you as you go forth in your career. Granted, this is just the start of your reference library.

1) Aristotle's *Poetics*
2) William Strunk and E.B. White—*The Elements of Style*
3) Lajos Egri—*The Art of Dramatic Writing*
4) Linda Seger—*Making A Good Script Great*
5) William Goldman—*Adventures in the Screen Trade*
6) Leslie Halliwell—*Halliwell's Film Guide*
7) Myrl Schreibman—*The Indie Producer's Handbook: Creative Producing from A-Z*
8) Mark Litwak—*Dealmaking for the Film and Television Industry*
9) Skip Press—*Writers Guide to Hollywood Producers, Directors, and Screenwriter's Agents*
10) *Leonard Maltin's 2010 Movie Guide*

SCREENWRITING COMPETITIONS

Whether you're a writer, a development executive, or a producer, it is important to keep up with the vast number of screenwriting competitions around the world. Some of the major ones go through an elaborate selection process, weeding out most of the mediocre screenplays by breaking down the initial submissions into quarter-finalists, semi-finalists, and finalists. While there are too many competitions to mention all of them, we have selected a few we feel the industry pays the most attention to:

- **Nicholl Fellowships in Screenwriting competition** (www.oscars.org/nicholl), sponsored by the Academy of Motion Picture Arts and Sciences, is an international competition, open to screenwriters who have not earned more than $5,000 writing for film or television. Entry scripts must be the original work of a sole author or of exactly two collaborative authors and must be written originally in English. Adaptations and translated scripts are not eligible. Up to five writers are awarded $30,000 fellowships each year. Agents, managers, studio execs as well as production company execs are keyed into this competition and receive lists of the finalists, including the quarter and semi-finalists. If a script moves through a few of these hoops, it will most likely be read by industry professionals prior to the announcement of the winner.

- **ABC** and **The Walt Disney Studios** (www.abctalent development.com) offer a one-year writing fellowship program in both television and motion pictures. There is no application fee, but they have strict guidelines so check out their Web site for details. Currently, it is a full-time program and if accepted, the writer will receive a salary for one year. In existence for fifteen years, their mission is to find new creative voices to work full-time developing their craft at The Walt Disney Studios and ABC Entertainment. While they accept up to eleven applicants, the exposure and education a writer will receive from this program would kick-start anyone's career.
- **The Samuel Goldwyn Writing Awards** (www.tft.ucla. edu/awards) is a college competition, offered to any enrolled student, undergraduate or graduate, attending any University of California campus for the winter, spring, and summer quarters.
- **Austin Film Festival** (www.austinfilmfestival.com) offers an opportunity for new writers to enter their work in a competition in either adult or family categories within a broad variety of genres including horror, sci-fi, romance, western or comedy. They also offer a teleplay competition for previously or currently produced episodic TV shows both hour and half-hour genres. Winners receive the Bronze Typewriter Award, win a cash prize, and are reimbursed travel and accommodations up to $500. The catch is that you must not have earned a living as a television or feature film writer. There is a small application fee and the winners are announced at the festival. Also, all finalists receive free tickets to the eleven-day festival, which kicks off with a four-day Heart of Film Screenwriters' Conference usually filled with panels and workshops with prominent writers, directors, producers, and executives.

- **Big Bear Lake International Film Festival Screenwriting Competition** (www.bigbearlakefilmfestival.com) is an up-and-coming film festival with an emphasis on new filmmakers. Their screenwriting competition has received recognition from many respected agents, managers, and producers. With a small application fee, the winners are announced at the festival in a very "Telluride-like" atmosphere nestled in the mountains two hours outside of Los Angeles.
- **Slamdance Screenwriting Competition** (www.slamdance.com/screencomp) offers comprehensive coverage on every script that is received. Readers choose fifty honorable mentions, thirty-five semi-finalists, and then the final top ten, from all the screenplays submitted. The winners are recognized at a Writers Guild of America reception in Los Angeles.

FILMMAKING LABS

- **The Sundance Institute** (www.institute.sundance.org). Sundance is more than just a film festival, it's a multi-disciplinary arts organization dedicated to the development of artists of independent vision as well as the showing of their new work. The Feature Film Program was created by the Institute in 1981 to support next-generation filmmakers, and has at its core the Screenwriting and Filmmaking Laboratories. They select fifteen to twenty projects each year in one or more areas.

   The Screenwriters Lab is a five-day writer's workshop that takes place in January and again in June. The program offers ten to twelve emerging artists the opportunity to work intensively on their feature film scripts with the support of established screenwriters.

   The Filmmakers Lab is a three-week hands-on workshop for writers and directors and occurs each June. Participants gain experience rehearsing, shooting, and editing scenes from their screenplays under the mentorship of accomplished directors, editors, cinematographers, and actors. The Institute provides airline travel, accommodations, and food for one writer/filmmaker per project. Check out their Web site for details regarding more than one filmmaker per project. Through open submissions as well as an on-going staff outreach to schools and film professionals, submitted screenplays go through a rigorous selection process conducted by staff and an advisory committee of filmmakers, writers, and independent producers. A thirty-dollar processing fee must accompany every submission.

In addition to the above labs, they also offer the annual Independent Producers Conference, a three-day, intensive workshop focusing on the professional and business aspects of independent film production such as marketing, financing, and distribution.

- **Film Independent** (www.filmindependent.org) Throughout the year FIND offers screenwriting, directing, and producing labs, taking place over a seven-week period in which a maximum of ten participants are chosen to develop their craft and meet film professionals who can help in the development of their careers. After paying a fifty-five dollar application fee per project for members and seventy-five for non-members, if selected, the workshop, seminar, and lab is free to the participant. The competition is fierce but anyone can attend the once-a-week seminars for any of the labs by paying a nominal fee (either per session or for the full seven weeks) and FIND members get a discount. The lab participants not only get the seminars but also attend two other nights of lab and workshops where they are mentored by indie professionals as they work diligently on their projects.

  FIND also offers inexpensive memberships. Members may attend free screenings and reasonably priced seminars, are given discounted admission to the Los Angeles Film Festival, and receive reduced rates for equipment, access to rooms for casting, use of the resource library, and help from mentors.

Both the Sundance Institute Labs and the FIND Labs have you sign a deal in which you give them a percentage should your film be produced as well as an acknowledgement in the credits. It's a small price to pay for such an education, support, and a "leg up" the ladder.

- **IFP (Independent Film Project)** (www.IFP.org) When FIND split from IFP a few years ago, it left two groups both offering the independent filmmaker a place to network, to learn and to be nurtured. FIND is in Los Angeles, but IFP has chapters in New York, Chicago, Minnesota, Phoenix and Seattle. It offers some of the same filmmaker friendly events and Labs that FIND does, as well as an Independent Filmmakers Conference and Independent Film Week in New York; Producers Workshop Series and Midwest Filmmakers Summit in Chicago; and Production Assistants Workshops in Phoenix. Celebrating its thirtieth anniversary, IFP has more than 10,000 members worldwide. Membership fees differ depending on which IFP you join so check out their website which is chalk full of information for the indie filmmakers.

FILM FESTIVALS

Film festivals offer a great opportunity for exposure, whether you're a filmmaker or an exec, as well as great prospects to network and meet new people. There are a number of Web sites offering information about film festivals—where they are, when they are, and how to submit, including Film Festivals Today (www.filmfestivaltoday.com) and Film Festivals (www.filmfestivals.com). Without A Box (www.withoutabox.com) is a great and easy resource for sending your films directly to film festivals.

The major film festivals such as Sundance, Cannes, Toronto, Venice, Berlin, Telluride, Los Angeles, Tribeca as well as Big Bear Lake International, Palm Springs International, Santa Barbara, Newport Beach, Slamdance, and Seattle, to name only a few, have their own Web sites.

GADGETS, GIZMOS, SOFTWARE, AND TOOLS OF THE TRADE

With technology reaching an all-time high, there are many programs and "toys" which can help you on your development path. While you don't need all these devices to succeed, they can make your life considerably more efficient.

- It is important to make sure that the screenplay is in proper format. There are many software programs which address this. There is no reason in the world for a screenplay to be submitted in a format that is unacceptable to industry standards. They are reasonably priced and are updated all the time, making the writing and formatting of a script more accessible to the average person. Software such as Final Draft, Movie Magic Screenwriter, and Hollywood Screenwriter provide professional looking screenplays for the well-seasoned writer or the novice just starting out.
- Having a Rolodex, whether computerized or a hard copy, which keeps track of all your contact information as well as a database (such as Filemaker Pro) enabling it to store names of talent, their

credits, and contact information, can be a valuable addition to your office.

- Handheld wireless devices and organizers such as the BlackBerry, Palm Pre, Google phone or the iPhone help busy industry execs stay connected. They not only include your address book and calendar, but are also connected to the Internet anywhere, anytime.

- If you are a producer, Entertainment Partners (EP) and Jungle Software's Gorilla offer both budgeting and scheduling software to break down screenplays in order to figure out, not only costs, but also how many days the shoot will last and, how many days you need each actor. However, a course in both scheduling and budgeting would be more than helpful to understand how to break down a screenplay in order to come up with a shooting schedule and budget. We also recommend Ralph Singleton's books on both scheduling and budgeting, especially for those who feel confident teaching themselves this process.

- The fact is for a mere $5,000, anyone can set up a mini movie studio these days. For less than $10,000, you can include some top equipment. This equipment might include a high-end Macintosh computer, a broadcast quality DV camera, Final Cut Pro or Avid Express (professional editing software), and possibly some other pieces of software for sound, mastering, and dubbing DVDs. If you use a PC, then Premiere is the editing software to use.

- Less technological but still a necessity are script brass fasteners also known as "brads." It is a mystery why some people do not invest in strong, sturdy brads. You have no idea what a pain it is to open a script and have it fall apart in your hands because the brads are cheap, thin, or bend too easily. Get the #5 solid brass fasteners, at least 1 1/4" long and only use two brads per script (leaving the middle hole empty). Do not be stingy on this. Brads matter. And whatever you do, don't bind a script and remember to only use a top and bottom brad, leaving the middle one empty.

- Another thing that goes hand-in-hand with the brads, is a rubber mallet. Yes, a mallet. Use the mallet to slam the brads down onto the script so as to flatten them and make sure that the sharp ends don't pierce the reader's hands or snag clothing. You may be laughing at this, but a poorly presented script can taint the reader's outlook before they even open the first page!

As technology changes to meet the needs of the industry, more "toys," gadgets, and software will emerge making everyone's jobs easier to accomplish.

COMPLETE LIST—INTERNET RESOURCE SITES

Some of these Web sites have basic service and some have additional services for a fee. Some have a great resource page of links to other useful sites which is quite helpful. We can't possibly list every Web site, what with all the new sites popping up all the time and others that are not updated or maintained. We also want to point out that we are not endorsing or advocating one over the other. However, these are some that we use ourselves. If we've missed any, feel free to drop us a line, and we'll include them in the next edition.

INDUSTRY SITES

ACADEMY PLAYERS DIRECTORY ....www.playersdirectory.com
Contact information for actors and actresses.

BASELINE STUDIOSYSTEMS ....www.studiosystem.com
Database for contacts, in-production and tracking.
Includes *Filmtracker*.

HOLLYWOOD CREATIVE DIRECTORY ....www.hcdonline.com
Fee-based database offering contact information, addresses
and phone numbers for industry companies.

INTERNET MOVIE DATABASE PRO ....www.imdbpro.com
Fee-based, more in-depth version of IMDB.

SHOWBIZ DATA ....www.showbizdata.com
Box office, industry search engines.

PUBLICATIONS

BILLBOARD MAGAZINE ....www.billboard.com
The end all trade paper for the music industry.

DAILY VARIETY ....www.Variety.com
Daily trade paper

FILMMAKER MAGAZINE ....www.filmmakermagazine.com
A quarterly magazine covering independent feature films
(this is included in your IFP membership).

HOLLYWOOD CREATIVE DIRECTORY ....www.hcdonline.com
Five contact directories, covering all aspects of the
professional industry.

THE HOLLYWOOD REPORTER ....www.HollywoodReporter.com
Daily trade paper.

KIRKUS REVIEWS...www.kirkusreviews.com
Twice-monthly publication which reviews books up to three
months prior to publication.

MOVIEMAKER MAGAZINE ....www.moviemaker.com
An international moviemaking magazine.

NIKKI FINKE'S DEADLINE
HOLLYWOOD DAILY.......................www.deadlinehollywooddaily.com
A blog dedicated to what is happening in Hollywood on a daily
basis. Nikki usually knows the info first before the trades.

PUBLISHERS WEEKLY ....www.publishersweekly.com
Weekly magazine reviewing books prior to their publication.

SCRIPT MAGAZINE....................................www.scriptmagazine.com
Provides information about the screenwriting industry.

STUDENT FILMMAKER MAGAZINE ....www.studentfilmmakers.com
A web site dedicated to student filmmaking.

TELEVISION WEEK ....www.tvweek.com
A weekly publication with subjects only related to
television news.

ORGANIZATIONS/GUILDS

ACADEMY OF MOTION PICTURE
ARTS AND SCIENCES..www.oscars.org

ACADEMY OF TELEVISION ARTS
AND SCIENCES ....www.emmys.org

ASSOCIATION OF TALENT AGENTS........www.agentassociation.com
This is a great free search engine to find what agent represents
what actor. No managers listed however.

DIRECTORS GUILD OF AMERICA ....www.dga.org

FILM INDEPENDENT (FIND) ....www.filmindependent.org

IFP ....www.ifp.org

PRODUCERS GUILD OF AMERICA ....www.producersguild.org

SAGIndie ....www.sagindie.com

SCREEN ACTORS GUILD ....www.sag.org

SCRIPTWRITERS NETWORK ....www.scriptwritersnetwork.org
A networking organization created by writers for writers

WRITERS GUILD OF AMERICA ....www.wga.org

RESEARCH SITES

ALL MUSIC GUIDE...www.allmusic.com
Database of artists and their labels, all music styles.

FILM INDUSTRY CENTRAL ....www.IndustryCentral.net
Advertises for professionals in the industry.

FILMMAKERS ....www.filmmakers.com
The art and showbiz of filmmaking; a resource for
filmmakers and screenwriters.

FILM STEW ....www.filmstew.com
Film Stew and Film Industry Central offer very complete
listings for film professionals.

HOLLYWOOD LIT SALES ....www.hollywoodlitsales.com
Lists the latest literary sales in Hollywood, updated daily.

HOLLYWOOD NET ....www.hollywoodnet.com
More links and lists and you can also communicate with
other filmmakers in list groups, subscribe to lists.

LYRICS...www.lyrics.com
Look up song lyrics to any number of songs.

LYRICS WORLD ....www.lyricsworld.com
Another database of song lyrics.

MANDY.COM...www.mandy.com
International film and TV production resources including
job listings.

MOVIEBYTES ....www.moviebytes.com
Something for everyone, "who's buying what?" winning
screenplays, agencies, etc.; premier site for screenplay contest
information.

MOVIE REVIEW QUERY ENGINE ....www.mrqe.com
Search engine listing movie reviews from different papers
for over 40,000 film titles.

WHO REPRESENTS ....www.whorepresents.com
Find the agent and/or manager that represents
specific talent for a small monthly fee.

BOOK WEB SITES

AUTHOR LINK...www.authorlink.com
The award-winning marketplace for the publishing industry,
where editors and agents buy and sell unpublished and
published manuscripts and screenplays. Providing *serious* writers
with access and exposure to the broadest range of legitimate
publishing professionals. Plus industry news.

AUTHOR'S DEN ....www.authorsden.com
A site dedicated to authors and readers.

PUBLISHERS MARKETPLACE aka
PUBLISHERS LUNCH ....www.publishersmarketplace.com
or www.publisherslunch.com
A dedicated marketplace for publishing professionals featuring
news, book deals, and a job board. You can receive a free daily
Publishers Lunch e-mail with highlights, use the Web site
limitedly, or pay a small monthly fee for greater access.

SCREENPLAY WEB SITES — Sites with Free Movie Screenplays

DAILY SCRIPT ....www.dailyscript.com

DREW'S SCRIPTORAMA ....www.script-o-rama.com

FREE SCREENPLAYS ....www.freemoviescripts.com

MOVIE SCRIPTS AND SCREENPLAYS
WEB RING HOME SITE ....www.moviescriptsandscreenplays.com
A bunch of movie scripts and screenplay sites in one location.

SCREENPLAYS FOR YOU ....www.sfy.ru
A Russian Web site with free movie screenplays.

SIMPLY SCRIPTS ....www.simplyscripts.com

FUN SITES

MOVIE MISTAKES..www.movie-mistakes.com

FINDING JOBS

ENTERTAINMENT CAREERS ....www.entertainmentcareers.net

ENTERTAINMENT JOBS NOW..........www.entertainmentjobsnow.com
All kinds, including below the line.

SHOWBIZ JOBS ....www. showbizjobs.com

FILM FESTIVALS

FILM BUZZ ....www.filmbuzzmarketing.com
Film Buzz is the first entertainment market research firm to
focus exclusively on independent motion pictures and is
uniquely positioned to offer its services at events where
filmmakers and distributors converge—film festivals.

FILM FESTIVAL TODAY ....www.filmfestivaltoday.com

FILM FESTIVALS..www.filmfestivals.com

FILM THREAT ....www.filmthreat.com
Web site that covers independent films. Created by Chris Gore,
the author of *The Ultimate Film Festival Survival Guide*, it has
become the bible for independent filmmakers hoping to launch
careers on the film festival circuit.

INDIEWIRE ....www.indiewire.com
Web Site and newsletter spotlighting the indie film community
since 1994 and includes the award-winning indieWIRE:DAILY
email newsletter, community postings, and free classifieds.

WITHOUT A BOX..www.withoutabox.com

LABS/FILM EDUCATION

AMERICAN FILM INSTITUTE ....www.afi.com
World-renowned AFI offers two-year master degree programs
in screenwriting, directing, producing, cinematography, editing,
and production design. They also offer the prestigious
Directing Workshop for Women.

ESE FILM WORKSHOPS
ONLINE ....www.esefilmworkshopsonline.com
Four to six week filmmaking and screenwriting courses that
provide a unique opportunity to learn the Ins and Outs of
today's Hollywood from industry professionals without
leaving your home.

FILM INDEPENDENT (FIND) ....www.filmindependent.org
Click on events and/or education. Used to be IFP but FIND
split from and became its own entity. Based in Los Angeles,
anyone can join by paying the membership fee. They offer
seminars, labs and workshops for the indie filmmaker.

IFP ....www.ifp.org
IFP offers educational seminars and workshops in New York
City, Minnesota, Chicago, Seattle and Phoenix. Each chapter
has its own activities and its own membership fees. New York is
the most active and sponsors Independent Film Week and the
Independent Film Conference that coincides with Indie Film
Week, offering five days of seminars and workshops. You can
also join as an interactive member to take part in podcasts and
use of info on the website. Every membership gets a subscription
to Filmmaker magazine.

LOS ANGELES FILM SCHOOL ....www.lafilm.com
L.A. Film School (LAFS) offers a one-year intensive filmmaking
workshop in the heart of Hollywood with concentration on
writing, directing, producing, cinematography, editing, sound
design, production design.

SUNDANCE INSTITUTE.......................................www.sundance.org
Click on programs.

UCLA EXTENSION ....www.uclaextension.edu
The Entertainment Studies program offers comprehensive
courses on the art and business of entertainment and offers
several certificate programs in film, television, and digital
entertainment media.

THE WORKSHOPS...www.theworkshops.com
Located in picturesque Rockport, Maine, this conservatory for
photography, filmmaking, video, and new media offers both
certificate and degree programs.

14

*"The Carrot May Be Dangling
but Someone's Got to Eat It!"*

that's a wrap!

By now, you are frustrated, excited, raring to go, and yet wondering where you're going. We have all had moments like that in our careers. You're not alone. First thing, get yourself a *Hollywood Creative Directory*, identify the companies that most interest you and send a letter with a résumé. Send lots of letters. Statistically, you will either be rejected or not even get a response—luckily you only need one response! If you are a student, you can offer your services as an intern for college credit. While you do not get paid usually, your foot will be in the door and that's a huge jump-start for a career. Temporary agencies offer administrative jobs within the industry and sometimes those jobs happen to be assisting a major player. Again, it's another way into the system. Find access to the UTA job list, human resource departments as well as trade papers—all of which can be of help. Networking with other assistants may also lead you to a job. You just need to find that first connection.

THE QUERY AND THE LETTER

So, how do you get yourself noticed? Is your résumé good enough? How do you write a letter that will garner attention? The following will offer some points to include in your letter and résumé that might help open some doors.

- Make sure your name, address, and phone number are clearly placed on the cover letter and resume.
- Make sure you spell the person's name you are sending your letter to correctly. As funny as that sounds, it's amazing how many letters we've gotten where our names are completely misspelled. It's too easy to dismiss a letter—don't make it even easier.
- The first paragraph should state briefly why you want to work at the company and what you have to offer.
- If you are trying to get someone to read a screenplay, give a genre, a logline, why it should be made, if it has placed in any screenplay competitions, and if there are any elements attached.
- If you are pitching a story, pitch one at a time. Do not write five loglines for the executive to choose from. Showing you have a lot of screenplays that have not sold does not help you sell that first one. Start with one, your best one!
- Be brief. Do not waste someone's time. Try to keep it to one page;
- Let them know that you will follow up with a phone call within two weeks.
- The résumé should include years, positions, company name, and a brief job description.
- Resumes should be tailor-made for each position. Be prepared to modify your résumé to fit the available job position.
- At the bottom of your resume, you should have your education, computer skills, and possible organizations, which might be of interest to an executive interviewing you.
- For a reader position, enclose a cover letter and three sample coverages of two scripts and one book. If at all possible, use something that is about to be made or a book you liked that might have been optioned. Remember to convey the story, make your points, and don't be afraid of your own opinion.

Assistant to President Sample Ad that was in Daily Variety

ASSISTANT TO THE PRESIDENT

Busy and exciting production company with offices in LA, NY and London seeks an assistant with the following skills:

- Windows, Word, Excel and Computer Proficient
- Able to work in an exciting but stressful environment
- Detail oriented with good organizational skills
- Muli-tasking, accurate, makes very few mistakes
- Good people skills
- Positive attitude
- Willing to travel

DO NOT APPLY if you:

- Are an actor
- Are thin-skinned, too sensitive, or your feelings hurt easily
- Can't work with temperamental creative types
- Want advancement, this job isn't for you
- Don't like working long hours
- Want a standard corporate structure
- Prefer family and social life over job
- Don't possess the skills required

PLEASE APPLY if you:

- Want to be the top assistant to an entrepreneur who is fun, exciting, a mover & shaker
- You like being the top assistant
- Are fast on your feet & can keep up with your boss
- Are solution oriented, not problem oriented
- Are willing to put in as many hours as it takes to get the job done
- Are not worried about family & social life
- Are looking for long-term employment

We would like to meet you if working for a company that rewards loyalty & dedication means something to you.
Good salary & benefits.
Please fax resume to:

SO NOW YOU'VE GOT THE JOB

When you get a job, even a temporary job, take it seriously and take extra steps required to be the best at it. How you handle tasks tells a lot about a person. Soak in as much information as you can and give more than just a hundred percent. Listen. Take care of your boss' needs. If you don't know something, say, "I don't know, but I'll find out right away." And then, *find out*—use your connections and contacts to find the information needed. If you make a mistake, don't make an excuse or cover it up. Humor is important as well. Get as much exposure as you can in the company you're working for. Take the extra initiative and offer your services to do coverage. Let them see how valuable you are. If you don't gamble on your instincts, no one else will. Find a mentor who can help advise you, should you need it. Above all, do the best work you can.

PATHS WE'VE TAKEN

Everybody has a different path in this industry. How each begins and where it leads will be different for every person. Nana Greenwald, former president of production at Kopelson Entertainment, began her career working in the opera. Now, she is entering the independent producer phase of her career. Joel Schumacher was a costume designer and is now a very successful and innovative film director. The list goes on. Learn from others and realize that the path you take is your own and, with it, brings your own perspective to the situations you face.

Monika's Path

Shortly after graduating from college, Monika began "temping" for Metromedia, KHJ-TV, advertising agencies, and radio stations, then got her foot in the door at Aaron Spelling Productions—where she once had to stand on a balcony and watch for Mr. Spelling to come out of dailies in order to tell her boss that Spelling was out so her boss could run down and talk to him.

Eventually, the temp jobs led her to an assignment at Paramount Pictures in the story department. She was exposed to the best screenplays that became some of the best movies made. When people would say, "You should read such and such script, it's really great!" She would do just that and get a sense and understanding of great writing. She worked around some of the most successful producers and executives, including those who were at the helm in those days: Barry Diller, Michael Eisner, Jeffrey Katzenberg, the late Don Simpson, and the late Dawn Steel.

She learned her job by doing and watching. The temp assignment eventually led to a permanent assistant position working for Lora Lee, who was the story editor at the time. When the Paramount studio break-up happened, Monika was offered the position of manager of the story department at Paramount Pictures by Dawn Steel. Instead, she followed her boss, Lora Lee, to Fox, to become the assistant story editor. Lora had been her mentor and Monika felt she still had more to learn from her. When Lora moved on to become a vice president at another company, Monika was promoted to story editor at Fox by Scott Rudin. Around the same time, Cari-Esta Albert, who was working at Universal Pictures, met with Monika—and the next thing she knew she was interviewing with Sean Daniel, who was then president of production at Universal Pictures. She jumped ship and moved to Universal Pictures where she spent ten years overseeing the story department. She was later promoted from executive story editor to vice president of creative and the story department by Casey Silver, president of production at the time.

At Universal, she worked under executives who are some of the top producers and executives today, including Sean Daniel, Casey Silver, Tom Pollock, Hal Lieberman, Nina Jacobson, Zanne Devine, to name a few. She set up and worked on a number of development projects there. One particular project she was instrumental in setting up was the action screenplay, *Black Dog*. After four years of development, it made it to the big screen starring Patrick Swayze. Monika carved a niche for herself by staying on top of screenwriting competitions, student filmmakers and their short films exhibited at film festivals like Sundance. Monika currently teaches feature film development at UCLA Extension, Riverside Community College's Distance Learning and taught a basic screenwriting course at the Dodge College of Film & Media Arts at Chapman University. She is the programming director for the Big Bear Lake International Film Festival as well as for the American Pavilion's Emerging Filmmaker Showcase at the Cannes Film Festival while continuing to guest lecture at various film festivals, film schools and workshops. She and Rona Edwards formed a production company as well as a script and film consultancy firm called Edwards Skerbelis Entertainment (ESE). Together, they develop scripts and nurture upcoming filmmakers and screenwriters. With several projects in active development, Monika was also recently associate producer on two movies (*Killer Hair* and *Hostile Makeover*) for the Lifetime Movie Network. She is the co-founder with Rona of ESE Film Workshops Online, a unique global online workshop that offers four to six-week courses on the ins and outs of the entertainment industry. Some of these courses include: "Maneuvering Film Festivals," "Creating a Production Company," "Finding & Developing New Ideas," and "Screenplay Development from the Inside Out."

Rona's Path

Rona's path was very different from Monika's path. She graduated from California Institute of the Arts with a BFA in theatre. She acted in a number of television shows, feature films, and commercials. However, she also had an affinity for filmmaking and writing. A friend asked if she would help do location scouting for a Saturday morning children's special. She replied, "Sure! What does a location scout do?" Being an actress, she thought movies just "got made." The answer was simple, they had the locations already and all she needed to do was get the release forms signed in the neighborhood. She hung around the set, spouting off her thoughts on film, whether people wanted to hear them or not. Two people liked what they were hearing...the producers, Emmy-Award winner Fern Field (*Heartsounds*, *Monk*) and her husband, Norman G. Brooks. They asked her to join their company as a development executive. When she told them she was an actress, they replied, "You can still act!" Famous last words...her path took a left turn. She worked at Brookfield Productions for a couple of years, setting up an Afterschool Special at ABC within the first two weeks of working there. She wrote two screenplays, which were both optioned, and did a documentary on Soviet kids who came to the United States to perform in a show called *Peace Child*. She went on to run John Larroquette's company, Port Street Films, where she co-produced *One Special Victory*, a movie for NBC, which starred the Emmy-Award winning actor, followed by a stint as vice president of creative affairs for Michael Phillips Productions (*The Sting*, *Close Encounters of the Third Kind*) in which she straddled the fence between feature film and television development. Realizing that development was a long and arduous journey, yet willing to embrace it anyway, and being a glutton for punishment, she decided to become an independent producer or rather was dragged kicking and screaming into the world of independent producing (though she now calls it "dependent producing"). In that time, she co-produced and/or executive produced *The Companion* (USA/Sci-Fi Channel), *I Know What You Did* (ABC), *Out of Sync* (VH1), and *Der Morder Meiner Mutter* (Sat.1/Studio Hamburg).

She set up *Matchmakers*, a feature at Warner Bros. based upon an article she found in a magazine and produced two movies for Lifetime based upon a series of mystery books she and Monika optioned subtitled

"Crimes of Fashion" by Ellen Byerrum. Starring Maggie (Psych) Lawson and Oscar nominee Mary McDonnell, *Killer Hair* and *Hostile Makeover* aired on the Lifetime Movie Network in 2009. She served as Executive Producer on the award-winning documentary, *Selling Sex in Heaven*, which won the Beyond Borders Media Award. Rona has had projects made and/or in development with many of the major networks and studios in both feature and television, including a script deal at ABC, movies at CBS, ABC, NBC, Hearst Entertainment, VH1, HBO, Lifetime, Lifetime Movie Network, Phoenix Television, Edward R. Pressman, Motor City Films, Warner Bros., Alan Landsberg Productions, The David Wolper Organization, All Girl Productions, and Wilshire Court, to name a few. She is also producing two more documentaries and has optioned several books while also developing a number of screenplays based upon her original ideas.

As a journalist, Rona has had hundreds of articles published in various publications. She is a contributing writer to *Produced By* magazine, the official magazine of the Producers Guild of America, had a column for seven years in *The Beachwood Voice*, and is currently writing a column for the *Neworld Review*, a New York newspaper in which she rants and raves about the film industry. Recently, she became a lifestyle columnist for the *Los Feliz Ledger* in Los Angeles.

In addition, Rona has been teaching "Introduction to Feature Film Development" at UCLA Extension for the past ten years and "Story Development Process in the Entertainment Industry" at Riverside Community College's Distance Learning program for the past four years. She also teaches at Chapman University's Dodge College of Film and

Tina Miller

Rona Edwards and Monika Skerbelis

Media Arts and has lectured, conducted workshops, and served on numerous film and screenwriting panels worldwide. With Monika, she is the co-founder of ESE Film Workshops Online, offering screenwriters and filmmakers an opportunity to learn the ins and outs of the film industry via online courses. The exciting thing for both Monika and Rona is that many of the alumni from ESE Film Workshops Online have gone on to win awards for their screenplays and films as well as obtain industry jobs due to their coaching and courses.

THE PATH NOT YET TAKEN

All this does is illustrate to you, the reader, that there is no set way, no set path on which to embark. You have to persevere, be vigilant, and do the work. Situations get thrown into your path which can steer you on a different course towards your goal...much like the structure of a screenplay. And, sometimes your goals change. But it is important to be aware of those obstacles and events that cross your path, to take full advantage of them, and to be prepared for the unexpected to happen.

You also must be careful how you present yourself. It is always better to be truthful. It's a small industry and it's too easy to discover someone is lying. For example: while at Universal, Monika received a letter and résumé from someone looking for a job. He stated in his résumé that he had worked in the Paramount story department with the dates corresponding to the exact dates she worked at Paramount. She never worked with him. When she called him and asked him about when he worked in the story department, his response was one of fumbling embarrassment as he admitted he had the wrong dates. It doesn't matter whether he lied or it was an error on his part, it left a mark—and not a good one! While some have made a career out of stretching the truth, we prefer to encourage you to always be as honest as you can. It works better for you in the long run and people rely on that, and are much more likely to trust you in the future.

Try to keep your focus—it is too easy in this business to scatter yourself all over the place and lose sight of the goals, passion, and the end results you have set your sights on. You have to keep a lot of balls in the air, granted, but don't lose the core of your passion.

Our paths have taken strange twists and turns. Recognizing such twists of fate has put us on paths that somehow run parallel to each other. We met through a mutual friend who felt that we would be simpatico. Over a networking lunch, we hit it off and have not only been friends but have worked together on various projects ever since. You never know how things will turn out but, most likely, the people you meet early on in your careers, who offer a support system and nurture you along the way, will be your friends for life.

CONCLUSION

Development is a word that extends beyond just a screenplay. The process can be scary. But, by now, you know the many pieces to the development puzzle—the players involved, how it works, and the process a screenplay goes through when it's first read, put into development, and then, hopefully, made into a film. It is a journey shared not just by the writer and producer, but by a number of creative people along the way. It is a path worth taking as long as you don't give up easily when the chips are down! You have to know when to push forward with a project and when to move on.

There are so many angles, so many strategies in order to achieve success in the development game. Hopefully, you've absorbed the many facets that are part of the development process. Facets such as pitching, finding ideas, and networking, as well as the players you deal with on a daily basis—whether a writer, reader, studio executive, production company executive, or an agent. Everyone shares a piece of the pie when it comes to development. The goals remain the same—to get a movie made!

Recognize your strengths to know where *you* fit into the puzzle. It's important to have a plan but just as important to be flexible. Sometimes the paths we start out on are not always the ones we end up taking, and yet you can still have great satisfaction knowing you are part of the big picture—making movies!

While this business can be a long hard climb, your chances are better than average if you have a good story. As long as you know who is who and are able to recognize good material, your chances of survival are greater than just knocking on doors alone.

Don't lose the dream! Don't let anyone dissuade you by telling you how impossible it is to get into this business. It's hard, but it's possible. The main thing is to soak up everything you can, love movies, be creative, assertive, and tell great stories. You will get kicked more often than not and no one will pat you on the back for a job well done. However, when you start climbing up the ladder, your skin will thicken and you'll be better equipped to handle the bumps in the road.

Good luck on your path, whatever it may be, and wherever it takes you!

sources used

Academy of Motion Picture Arts and Sciences, Margaret Herrick Library.

Balio, Tino. *History of the American Cinema: Grand Design: Hollywood as a Modern Business Enterprise, 1930-1939*. Scribner, 1993.

Bertsch, Marguerite. *How to Write for Moving Pictures A Manual of Instruction and information*. George H. Doran Company, 1917.

Beverly Hills Public Library.

Bower, Eileen. *The Transformation of Cinema, 1907-1915, Vol. 2*. Berkeley: University of California Press, 1994.

Caine, Clarence J. *How to Write a Photo Play*. David McKay Publisher, 1915.

Canton, Maj. *Maj Canton's Complete Reference Guide to Movies and Mini-Series Made for Television and Cable 1984-1994*. Adams-Blake Publishing, 1994.

Crowther, Bosley. *Hollywood Rajah: The Life and Times of Louis B. Mayer*. Holt, Rinehart and Winston, 1960.

Dimick, Howard T. *Modern Photoplay Writing It's Craftmanship*. James Knapp Reeve, Publisher, 1922.

Emerson, John & Loos, Anita. *How to Write Photoplays*. James A. McCann Co. Publishers, 1920.

Emerson, John & Loos, Anita. *Breaking Into the Movies*. James A. McCann Co., 1921.

Fawcett, L'Estrange. *Writing For the Films*. London Sir Isaac, Pitman & Sons, Ltd., 1932.

Francke, Lizzie. *Script Girls: Women Screenwriters in Hollywood*. British Film Institute, 1994.

Gordon, William Lewis. *How To Write Moving Picture Plays*. Atlas Publishing Company, 1915.

Gordon, W. L. *How to Write Photoplays*. The Writers Digest, 1921.

Hampton, Benjamin. *A History of the Movies*. Covici, Friede Publishers, 1931.

Henderson, Robert M. *D.W. Griffith His Life and Work*. Garland Publishing Inc., 1985.

Lewis, Howard T. *The Motion Picture Industry*. D. Van Nostrand, 1933.

Lytton, Grace. *Scenario Writing Today*. Houghton Mifflin Co., 1921.

Macgowan, Kenneth. *Behind the Screen: The History and Techniques of Motion Picture*. Delacorte Press, 1965.

MacCann, Richard Dyer. *The First Tycoons*. Scarecrow Press, 1987.

Marion, Francis. *How to Write and Sell Movie Stories*. Covici Friede Publishers, 1937.

Marell, Alvin H. *Movies Made for Television 1964-1986*. A Baseline Book/New York Zoetrope, 1982.

Moving Picture World. (Licensed Film Stories) Vol. 9, No. 2. July 22, 1911.

Muddle, E.J. *Picture Plays and How to Write Them*. Picture Play Agency, 1911.

Museum of Television and Radio.

Musser, Charles. *The Emergence of Cinema: The American Screen to 1907. History of American Cinema, Vol. 1*. New York: Charles Scribner's Sons, 1990.

Nelson, J. Arthur. *Photo-Play, Photoplay*. Publishing Company, 2nd edition, 1913.

Palmer, Frederick. *Palmer Plan Handbook: Photoplay Writing Simplified and Explained: a practical treatise on scenario writing, as practiced at leading motion picture studios*, Palmer Photoplay Corp., 1918.

Parsons, Louella O. *How to Write for the Movies*. A.C. McClurg & Co., 1915.

Ramsaye, Terry. *A Million and One Nights—History of the Motion Picture*. Simon & Schuster, 1926.

Schwartz, Nancy Lynn. *The Hollywood Writers' Wars*. Knopf, 1982.

Staiger, Janet. *The Studio System*. Rutgers University Press, 1995.

Thomas, A.W. *How to Write a Photoplay*. The Photoplaywrights' Association of America, 1914.

Thomas, Bob. *Thalberg: Life and Legend*. Doubleday, 1969.

University of California Los Angeles Research Library.

Wheaton, Christopher D., PhD. *A History of the Screen Writers Guild (1920-1942)*. USC Dissertation, 1973.

Writers Guild of America Library.

"I loved it (didn't just like it). This book literally explains everything an aspiring screenwriter or filmmaker needs to know, and in a way that's constructive, specific, and consistently interesting to read. Rona and Monika have a voice that engages you without being patronizing, that informs you without being stodgy, that enlightens you without being over your head."

> — David Madden, Executive Vice President,
> Fox Television Studios, Producer,
> *Save the Last Dance, Something The Lord Made*

"Now the frustrated writer who comes so close to selling their screenplay will understand the ins and outs of Hollywood and will be better equipped to achieving their goals. A must read for anyone starting out in the business."

> — Valerie McCaffrey, Casting Director,
> *American History X, Babe, The Legend of 1900*

"Skerbelis and Edwards offer down-to-earth advice that will help producers understand and cut through the sometimes arcane world of development."

> — Rosanne Korenberg, Producer,
> *Half Nelson, Hard Candy*

"Before you write or direct your dream project, buy this book. It will guide you through the maze of Hollywood, making it easier to navigate and comprehend what lies ahead. The perfect gift for every film school graduate."

> — Robin Schreer, Agent, The Mirisch Agency

"In *I Liked It, Didn't Love It*, Rona and Monika provide an excellent introduction for anyone pursuing a career in the idiosyncratic and exciting world of feature film development. A thorough and professional guide for the aspiring mogul, this book covers all the basics that every D-person in training must know."

> — Carr D'Angelo, Producer, *The Animal, The Hot Chick*

"*I Liked It, Didn't Love It* is a must-read for emerging writers, directors, producers, and aspiring studio, network, and cable TV executives. Former Universal Pictures VP Monika Skerbelis and producer Rona Edwards demystify the circuitous path to development and production."

> — Harrison Reiner, CBS Staff Story Analyst; UCLA
> Instructor of Screenwriting and Story Development

"With *I Liked It, Didn't Love It* Monika Skerbelis and Rona Edwards provide a valuable road map to a career in the motion picture development. Everybody has to start somewhere and this is a better place than most."

> — Barry Isaacson, Former Universal Pictures
> Studio Executive